I Don't Have Time For Green Bananas

An Unripe Memoir

Written By
Tracey Fuller

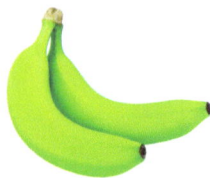

"Tracey darling, I don't have time for green bananas. Put them back!"

-Barbara Fuller, 93 years old

Dedicated to Grammy

Table of Contents

Annual Physical

I hoisted myself onto the exam table and tore the paper cover with my ass. On the wall in front of me hung a framed diploma from Columbia University with *cum laude* inscribed in gold ink. Smart guy, I thought.

Knock. Knock. "Come in," I said, shivering and impatient. Dr. Young was... young. He was statuesque with wavy brown hair, green eyes and olive skin.

"What are you here for?" he asked.

"Over an hour, I think," I gave him a look.

"I'm sorry you had to wait so long," he said, flipping through my paperwork.

"Look, Dr. Young, I said, "I'm sixty! How am I supposed to remember my entire medical history? Who cares when I had my last tetanus shot? If I get punctured by a rusty nail, I'll get another one."

"Tracey," he said, affectionately patting my shoulder. "You're gonna be..."

I interrupted him mid-sentence. "Dr. Young, when this physical is over will you be giving me a diagnosis?"

"Not likely, why?"

"Because these days I get second opinions from Web MD."

"Very funny, Tracey." He placed the clipboard on the counter. "Please, no Web MD. It only complicates things. You'll be outta here soon," he promised.

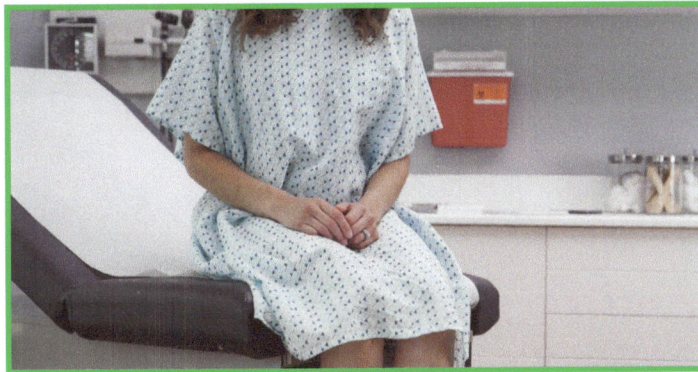

"Green banana soon?"

"What?" he asked, confused.

"Nothing," I mumbled. "It's a figure of speech."

Dr. Young looked me over from head to toe. "Everything looks fine." He pulled off his gloves. "Go home and scan your medical records."

"Wait, what?"

"Create an electronic file of your medical records and get on with your life."

"Easy for you to say, Doctor Y-O-U-N-G." I enunciated every letter.

"You're quibbling over semantics, Tracey. It's just my name."

"Wish it were mine." Wink. Wink.

Fitbit

My kids gave me a Fitbit for Christmas, but I wanted an Apple watch.

"Geez, kids," I said, "you shouldn't have." And I meant it. Disappointed but not ungrateful, I thanked them. "Am I supposed to wear it all the time, or just when I exercise?"

"All the time is better, Mom," said my son-in-law. "It will track your sleep, remind you to move, and it's water-proof. We know how much you love to swim."

"Ya know, kids, there's a name for someone who tracks your every move."

"What?" they asked in unison.

"A stalker! So I'm naming my stalker—Fit Bitch."

I kissed all four adult children goodbye and thanked them for their 'thoughtful' gift. A week or two later, the family reunited for a long weekend. While we walked the perimeter of the golf course, my daughter noticed that I wasn't wearing Fit Bitch. "Where's your Fitbit, Mom?" asked my daughter.

"It's in the drawer next to my Forever stamps."

"Why is it next to your Forever stamps, Mom?"

"Because nothing lasts forever, so that's where she belonged. Did you know that Forever stamps are going up three cents next year?"

"No, but the price of stamps is always going up."

"Then forever isn't forever," I said. "Is it?"

"Can I have it?" asked Amy. "Mine is old."

"Of course you can." I headed to the drawer where I had stowed it away.

I removed the device from the drawer and placed it on Amy's wrist. "Thanks, Mom."

"You're welcome, Honey," I smiled. "I don't mean to sound ungrateful Amy, but the next time you buy me a device to wear to bed—make sure it vibrates!"

My Naked Body

A few days ago, I stood naked in front of a mirror. What a sight! I had never noticed the roundness of my belly or my turned-out foot. My forehead was slightly smaller than I'd imagined, my neck shorter than Audrey Hepburn's, and my cheeks plumper than Alfred Hitchcock's. My butt was so flat and wide, I was certain I could balance a glass of wine on it.

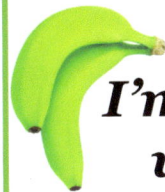

> *I'm pear-shaped with an uber flat-ass and large peaches.*

So, I decided to take my measurements: waist, thigh, and hip, and then hire a personal trainer.

The proper pronunciation of my trainer's name was Michelle, but I called her Miss Hell. She had rock-solid abs and a tiny round ass. I hated that fit bitch. Forgive me, I mean *envied* her.

I brought my stats to our first session. "Check out these numbers." I was mortified. "First of all, I'm pear-shaped with an uber flat-ass and large peaches. Can you give me a figure like Jane Fonda? I don't have time for green bananas."

"You talk like you're a bowl of fruit, Tracey," she said. "I'll keep you fresh."

"That's very clever, Michelle." I acknowledged her wit. "I appreciate that."

We proceeded on a bi-weekly routine of interval training, TRX core work, and Kinesis wall exercises. Within the first ten minutes of each session, I was begging for mercy.

"Miss Hell," I'd yell, "can I stop now?"

"Lower your voice, Tracey. People will think I'm hurting you."

"You *are* hurting me."

After my workouts, I'd soak in a tub of Epsom Salts. Like a submarine diving into the depths of the ocean, I'd submerge myself into the dissolving crystals and feel each muscle begin to relax. The only place I could straighten my right foot was in the bathtub by pressing my big toe into the spigot. It's amazing how nothing ever hurts in a bathtub.

I am not inclined to stare at my naked body again, but if I do, I hope I'll be pinching myself on the cheek, or the butt, whichever looks better.

Stop Thinking and Start Doing

I recently asked Jim to provide some encouragement while I grappled with retirement. Here is how that conversation went.

"Babe," I said during pillow talk, "I read that scheduling one's day is far more productive than winging it, especially in retirement. We have so many hours to fill. Will you help me plan a routine?"

"Forget it. It sounds like work."

"But I need your encouragement," I pouted.

"Okay, Tracey. Then I encourage you to stop thinking and start doing."

"Do what?" I asked. "I'm trying to arrange my day so that I'm the most productive."

"Why are you so compelled to be productive now? You're retired."

"Because retired people need routines and a sense of purpose. I'm at a loss. Will you help me?"

"No. It's Men's Day and I'm golfing."

"Fine. I'll go for a walk."

"Bye," he said, pursing his lips for a kiss.

I kissed Jim goodbye, then slipped into my gym clothes and walked three times around my cul-de-sac. Once home, I needed another plan so I called Pam. "Hey Pam, are you free for lunch today?"

"No, Tray. Sorry. I'm so busy."

"Doing what?"

"I played pickleball this morning. I'm meeting Steve for lunch after his golf game. I have a two o'clock facial, and in between, I have to run home to walk the dog and check on the remodel. Then at four, I'm consignment shopping with my designer."

"What about tomorrow?"

"Sorry, I can't. I'm busy all week. Workmen come and go all day. Let's try in May when I'll have more time."

"May?" I said, raising my voice.

At that point, I realized I needed a Pam-kind-of-life. So, I concocted a plan and would tell Jim about it when he got home.

"Jim, I figured out what I'm going to do to be productive."

"What?" he asked skeptically.

"Remember this morning when you told me to stop thinking and start doing?"

"Yes." He rolled his eyes. "So, what are you going to do, Tray?"

"I am going to take pickleball lessons, arrange a series of massages and facials, get a dog and remodel the house."

"Oh shit!" he said regrettfully. "Maybe I should rethink this."

Inventor-in-Chief

I consider myself to be an inventor-in-chief; however, I have been repeatedly rejected while attempting to protect my intellectual property. For instance, in December 2018, I tried to trademark the phrase, 'I Don't Have Time for Green Bananas.' Months later I received a response that read: 'the applied-for mark is a widely used commonplace expression.' What a rotten outcome! (pun intended)

In 1989, I painted adorable pictures on my daughters' tennis shoes so they could discern left from right. When the shoes were placed on the correct feet, the image was complete. Bingo! Problem solved.

When I tried to patent the left/right shoe puzzle concept, I was denied because a supposed similar patent had been approved in 1959, whereby a person could place half of a sticker with an image on it inside of each shoe. Another rotten outcome. And, might I add, TOTALLY different from my artistic solution to the age-old shoe dilemma!

Who cares about trademarks and patents anyway? I was the inventor-in-chief, determined to persevere. So, I decided to contact the largest shoe manufacturer in the country, Buster Brown. The executives were interested. They flew me to St. Louis first-class. My Shoe Puzzles were a hit. In a market study, they surpassed Keds and Sketchers for kids' favorite shoes.

Ultimately, Buster Brown could not figure out how stores with limited shelf space could display two shoes instead of one. Half of a dolphin could be a tough sell. Such a rotten outcome.

For the next three years, I continued to paint Shoe Puzzles and sold them in LA boutiques: Pixie Town, Nordstrom's, Fred Segal, and others. Today, shoes with opposing images or phrases are sold everywhere. A sales associate simply pulls out a smartphone and shows the customer the mate. I clearly was ahead of my time.

Years later, I invented the Beach Sheet, a king-sized sheet with sand-pocket corners that converts into a backpack for a hands-free walk along the beach. I never tried to trademark or patent the Beach Sheet, but there's still time. Shark Tank anyone?

I also had an idea for a board game that I called Catch-up Mustard. It was modeled after the popular game Chutes and Ladders, only messier. Ha-ha.

Any more clever inventions, you ask?

Just give me time.

Brazilian Blowout

One summer, I was in Beaver Creek, Colorado, and could not manage my thick frizzy hair. So, I decided to visit a hair salon in the Westin hotel. For the first ten minutes, I described my hair horrors to the stylist. In the following ten minutes, I listened to her tell me about the brilliance of a Brazilian Blowout. "See how your hair is thick, curly, and frizzy?" she said, grabbing a clump of my hair. "I can fix that in no time."

"No time?" I mimicked. "Really? What's your definition of no time? I have an event tonight and need to pick up my outfit at the dry cleaners. They close at six. It's three now."

"More than an hour, less than two," she said.

"Do it."

An assistant began by shampooing my hair with an anti-residue product. Then, the blow-out. "Wow!" I said. "That was fast, but I can't leave the salon looking like this." Imagine Don King.

"We're not done, Tracey." She stirred a toxic-smelling potion that she began combing through my hair. My eyes burned. I began to cough uncontrollably.

"Is that stuff safe?" I asked.

"Totally safe," she said. "Want some water?"

By then, I was choking on the foul-smelling air. "Yes, I'd love some, but I might need something stronger. Do you have an antidote for this stuff?"

"What's that?" she asked.

"A medicine that's given to counteract poison." She shrugged off the comment, then escorted me to the washbasin. "Thank God you're rinsing it out," I said. "But why ruin it? My hair is finally straight."

"You'll see," she said, drowning my ears in water.

After the final blow-out, I leaned in close to the mirror. "Cher, is that you?" I blinked a few times to focus on my image.

"OMG, I have Cher hair."

I paid the young stylist hundreds of dollars before rushing to the cleaners.

They were closed.

7

Kick the Bucket List

What should I have on my bucket list? I don't know.

So, I decided to ask Nina, my Vietnamese manicurist, while she was doing my nails.

"Nina," I said, fingers splayed on the table.

"Do you have a bucket list?"

"What's that?"

"It's a grocery list of things you want to do before you die."

"Are you dying?"

"No, well…" I stumbled. "Eventually. But there's stuff I want to do and I'm already sixty."

"Like what?"

"Like publishing a book and traveling to exotic parts of the world. Stuff like that."

"Why do you need a list?" she asked, drizzling oil on my nailbed.

"To check off the stuff on the list."

"Oh, so like if you travel to somewhere like Vietnam you can cross that off your list?"

"Yes," I said, thrilled that she understood. "Kind of ironic, right? To actually need a list."

"What's that?" she asked, artfully polishing my pinkie nail.

"What's what?"

"I-run-Nick?"

"I didn't say I-run-Nick," I clarified. "I said ironic." I pronounced it slower this time.

"That's what I said, Tracey," Nina repeated. "I-run-Nick."

"Are you done?" I said, rising from my chair. "I need to talk to my therapist."

I left the salon with wet nails, drove straight to my travel agent, and booked a trip to Vietnam.

I like the way Nina thinks.

8

Ancestry Dot Calm

I decided to follow millions of people curious about their familial relations by submitting my DNA to Ancestry.com. Who knows, I thought, I might be of royal descent. Princess Tracey—it has a nice ring to it, right?

In the eighties, I dreamt that I was related to Princess Diana because our hair was exactly the same. We were twinsies, in my mind. Also, someone once told me that I looked like Kristen Wiig and that I was just as funny as she is. "Are you two related?" they'd ask. "I don't know," I'd say. "Maybe."

Anyway, I decided to mail in my DNA. Then I waited. And waited. And waited.

Six weeks later an email arrived. It read, 'Due to high demand, our lab is a little behind schedule. But rest assured—your DNA kit has been received, we are working diligently to deliver your results, and we will send you an email once processing begins. Thank you for your patience!'

Patience? I'm not patient. I'm the green banana lady. If I die before I find out that I'm related to Princess Di I'll be devastated. Actually, I'll be dead so it won't matter. But, it might matter to my daughters. They would want to know if they were royalty or not.

Princess Tracey was running out of time.

Eight weeks later, my DNA was revealed.

Drum roll, please.

94% European Jew, 4% Europe South, and 2% Green Banana.

These results are 100% dull as dishwater, except the 2%.

Long live the green banana lady!

Loser Girl

After a two-year hiatus from Facebook, I decided to return to the world of social media and try my best to share stories with all of you. It was confusing, so I consulted a friend.

"Linda," I said, "I have a bunch of green banana stories that I'd like to share with people, but I don't know how."

"Are you on Facebook?"

"Not anymore."

"Why not?"

"Because I suffer from click-phobia."

"Huh?" she said. "What the fuck is click-phobia?"

"Fear of clicking," I explained. "I'm afraid that I might click on something and end up in a world of talking animals."

"Are you out of your mind?" she shouted.

"Yes," I whined. "Please help me." Linda watched as I booted up my Mac and opened Facebook.

"Username?" she asked.

"Green Bananas?" I suggested. "That would be awesome."

"No, Tracey. You need a real username."

"Okay, fine. I'll try Tracey Fuller." I typed in my name. "It's taken, Linda, now what?"

"Use an alias," she suggested.

"What about Mrs. Green Bananas? I love that username."

Discouraged, Linda said, "What do you want as your cover photo?"

"Are green bananas okay, or do I need a picture of me?"

"People prefer pictures of people," she said, as though it were obvious.

"Then I want green bananas," I insisted, "because that's my rebellious side."

An hour later, Linda left me alone staring at my monitor. Click. Click. Click. I made three Facebook friends, then suddenly, something went very wrong. Inadvertently, my mouse hovered over the acronym GIF. I must have clicked it. Guess what popped up?

Loser Girl.

Robocall

I was in the middle of preparing Ina Garten's chicken parmesan when suddenly my landline rang. In general, I resist answering my landline because every call is a robocall. Nonetheless, I had a little wine in me, so I answered it.

A familiar-sounding female voice said, "There are serious allegations against you. Get back to us so we can discuss this matter before taking any legal action."

"Jim!" I yelled across the house. "Are you involved in a nefarious business deal?"

"What are you talking about, Tracey?"

"I just answered the landline and the female voice sounded suspiciously like my mom. She threatened legal action if I didn't call her back."

"Your mom has been dead for eight years, Tracey. It was a robocall, just ignore it."

I let it go.

Two days later, I was whipping up Ina's orecchiette with broccoli rabe and sausage dish, merrily sipping the remainder of my Roar Pinot Noir when the landline rang again. In my wine fog, I picked up the phone. "Hello."

"Can you hear me?" said a female voice.

Again, it sounded eerily like my deceased mom.

"Ma? Is that you?" The voice freaked me out. I hung up.

"Jim," I said, setting the dinner table, "you'll never guess who called."

"Who?"

"My mom. I think she's haunting me from the grave. First, she threatened to sue me, then she made me feel like I ignored her."

"Why would she do that?" he asked while refilling my wine glass.

"Control," I said emphatically. "She always has to control everything."

We lit a few candles, toasted to our fabulous dinner, and savored our pasta. Once again, the landline rang.

"Do not answer that," Jim insisted.

"What if it's my mom?"

"You'll call her back after dinner."

Cemetery Walk

I visited my friend Samira at her new town-home in Santa Monica. She and her adorable dog Morton live a block away from a cemetery. It was a beautiful afternoon, so we decided to take Morton for a walk.

As we strolled past the graveyard gates, I asked Samira, "Do you ever walk Morton in the cemetery?"

"Nope," she said, "Morton senses death."

"Does that mean Morton won't poop on cemetery grass? You're going to clean up after him anyway, right?"

"Of course," she said, defending the sensitive pup. "Maybe Morton thinks I'll die if I walk through the cemetery gates."

"Doubtful," I said.

Morton pooped outside the graveyard gates, and Samira scooped it into a plastic bag. When she spotted a trashcan just inside the cemetery walls, Samira tugged at Morton's leash to get him through the gates. Morton wouldn't budge.

"Morton, come!" Samira demanded. He wouldn't move.

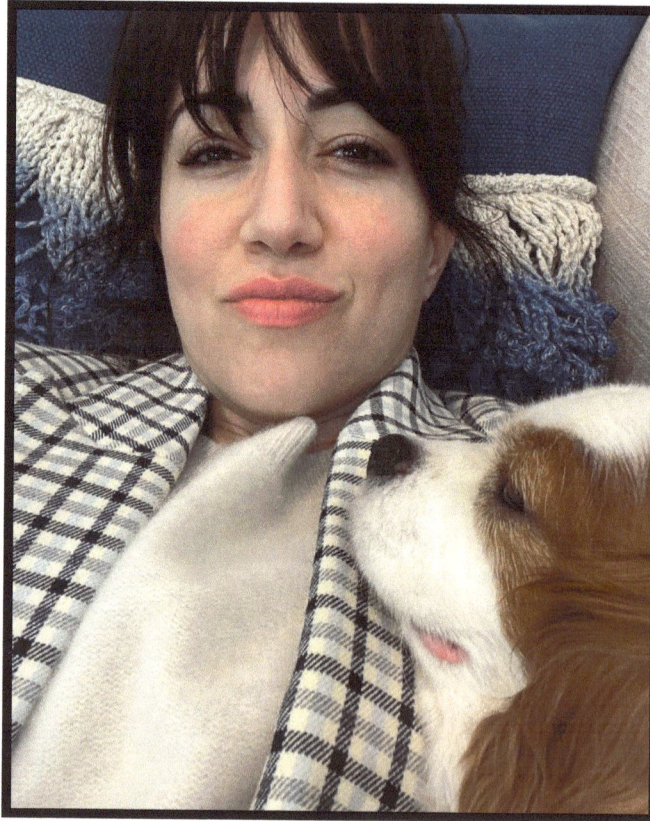

"I bet he'll go with me. We have no attachments. Give me his leash and I'll show you."

Samira handed me Morton's leash, and we walked through the cemetery gates.

"Wow!" she squealed. "That's unbelievable. He's never gone in there with me."

I flung the shit into the trashcan, strolled out through the gates, and handed her back the leash.

"Mission accomplished," I boasted. "Obviously, Morton doesn't care if I die."

"Good boy," said Samira, petting her dutiful dog.

"What's good about it?" I questioned. "Your sensitive dog just escorted me to my grave."

"No he didn't, Tracey. He just had a breakthrough moment."

"No shit," I said sarcastically, "leave it to a dog."

Ruff.

Mother's Day with Mom

"Hey, Mom," I said, standing graveside, "I brought you a bunch of green bananas for Mother's Day. You'd be so proud of me. I'm keeping your memory alive by writing stories about the urgency we feel while aging. I'm sharing them on Facebook. People love 'em."

"That's nice, Darling," she said, snickering a bit. "But what I'd really like for Mother's Day is the Neiman Marcus catalog."

"What do you want from Neiman's?"

"A pink Chanel Flap," she said without hesitation.

"Mom, what do you want that for?"

"Please Darling, don't argue with me. The lady next to me has dozens of Chanel handbags. You'd better bring me Bergdorf's catalog, too."

"What is going on down there, Mom?

You look stunning. You're wearing your pink St. John suit, your rose petal Gucci scarf, and your black-tipped Chanel tan flats."

"Tracey, darling," she said sassily, "a 'classy lady' needs a classy bag."

"Mom, how did you know that we put 'A Classy Lady' on your gravestone?"

"I read it!"

"No way, Mom. That's creepy."

"It's only creepy if I don't live up to it. Now go home and bring me both catalogs."

"Can't I just buy you a handbag?"

"No!" she yelled impatiently. "I need a few other things."

"What other things?"

"Don't ask," she said, perturbed. "I'm buried next to Coco Chanel."

Meghan and Harry

Last night, in their royal boudoir at Nottingham Palace, the Duke and Duchess of Sussex consummated their marriage. Here is my account of what took place.

"Harry, my prince," sighed Meghan, "I don't have time for green bananas."

"I'm not sure I understand what you mean, my love. Why don't you take off your bustier, and we can discuss it."

"I'm serious Harry. I'm 36 years old. I need to conceive on our wedding night."

Meghan slowly unwound the laces of her bustier while Harry daintily removed her garter. Unhurriedly, he slid each nylon down her long slender legs. Meghan now stood naked before her prince.

"Harry," she sighed, "this won't work unless you take off your clothes too."

"I know my duchess, but I've waited my entire life for this moment and I'd like to savor it for a while."

"How long is a while?" Meghan shrugged her bare shoulders.

"I'll let you know," said Harry, "but not now."

Harry gazed at her sparkling brown eyes, then her lips, breasts, waist, and finally...

"Are you feeling okay, Harry?" You're acting strange. What's wrong?"

"I'm feeling a bit off-color, darling. It's been a long day. I'll be okay in a few minutes. You are so beautiful. I'm the luckiest man in the world." Harry went back to admiring his bare bride.

A few minutes later Meghan asked, "May I take your shirt off for you, Harry? I think you'll be more comfortable."

"Yes, my love. You may take off my shirt." Meghan unbuttoned Harry's shirt and tossed it onto a chair. "I feel better now sweetheart. That was a splendid idea."

"May I remove your pants for you?"

"Not yet, Darling."

"Why not?"

"Because," he said, "my banana is green."

Figuratively, my darling," said Harry. "What I mean is, if we try to conceive now, I am worried you will end up giving birth to a plantain.

"You have a green banana, Harry?" gasped Meghan. "What on earth do you mean?"

"Figuratively, my darling," said Harry. "What I mean is, if we try to conceive now, I am worried you will end up giving birth to a plantain."

Just then Meghan ripped off Harry's pants and they royally made love.

Nine months later, Meghan gave birth to an adorable baby boy, and the whole bunch lived happily ever after.

Honoring Dad

My father-in-law left an indelible mark on my heart. I called him Dad. This exchange happened on Memorial Day, 2001.

"Tracey, come here," he said. We were both in the garage at the time.

"Eeny, meeny, miny, mo," I mumbled pointing to his wall of hats.

"You can't wear my hats," he growled.

"Why not, Dad? I left mine at home."

"Because I have a big head. They won't fit."

"Can't I just try one?" I begged.

"No," he said, "not even one."

On the wall of the garage, next to his workbench, Dad hung a dozen hats: Air Force, Yankees, Sailor, Straw. You name it, he had it. They were tempting as chocolate.

"I promise I'll hang it up right where I found it," I assured him.

"No, Tracey. Come over here, I want to show you something." I walked over to his workbench and peered over his shoulder. He was gluing parts onto a model airplane. It was his third model airplane. The others dangled from long wires above his workbench. "I flew this plane in WWII," he said, holding up the grey plastic model. Dad pointed to the cockpit where he sat, then to the compartment that held the bombardier. "I led 25 missions over Germany. I lost a lot of friends." I wrapped my arms around his burly back and kissed his soft round head.

"That must have been very difficult for you, especially when you reflect upon it today. Wanna talk about it, Dad? I'd love to hear about your service in the Air Force."

"No. I just wanted you to see my model airplane."

"It's great, Dad. Your attention to detail is flawless. You have such a steady hand. Not many men your age would tackle such intricate model airplanes. Your work is fantastic."

Dad was 80 years old. He had recently been diagnosed with prostate cancer. He rarely spoke of his years in the Air Force. I remained quiet, hoping he might finally share his story.

"I served in the 8th Air Force, 305th Bomb Group and was awarded the Distinguished Flying Cross and the Air Medal with three oak leaf clusters."

"You really served our country in the most profound way, Dad. I couldn't be more proud."

"It wasn't easy, kid," he said backing up his chair. "My group always flew in formation. My B-17 was in the lead position. We dropped bombs on enemy targets. Most missions left me with a pit in my stomach that remains with me to this day."

"You obeyed orders, Dad. You were battling a horrific war. A war that had to be fought. A war we finally won."

"Doesn't make it easy, kid. Those were tough times."

"Imagine a world where brave men and women were too afraid to fight for their country and for our freedom as American citizens."

"Were you afraid?"

"Afraid of what?" He raised his shoulder.

"Of dying?"

"Never. There was no time to be afraid. It was business, as usual, every time I entered the cockpit."

"But you're human. You must have been afraid. Fear is a natural emotion."

"Not when you're a fighter pilot in wartime with millions of lives relying on you to do your job."

"That's intense. The depth of your bravery, under those circumstances, is unimaginable."

"Imagine a world, Tracey, where brave men and women were too afraid to fight for their country and for our freedom as American citizens."

"I hope that day never comes, Dad. Today, and every day, I will honor you and all the brave men and women who serve our country. I will never forget what you did for our freedom."

On October 6th, 2003, Dad passed away. Three airplanes floated above the workbench in his garage. Painted in bright red across the front of that last model airplane was written the word, "Fearless."

Dad was right about the size of his head. I was right about the size of his heart.

Computer Updates

I entered the bright white Apple store feeling dull grey. I was the fifth person in line, so I passed the time by playing Words with Friends and searching for Duck a l'orange recipes. Just a craving, that's all. A young man wearing a red cap came up to me and asked, "Are you Tracey Fuller?"

"Yes," I said, "Tracey with an 'e' that's me!"

He dilly-dallied on his iPad for a minute, then asked, "What can I help you with today?"

I handed him my Mac. "Beach balls! I need you to get rid of the spinning beach balls."

"What do you mean?" he said, opening my computer.

"I mean the High Sierra update has caused beach balls to spin all over my Mac. I'd like the Low Sierra back, please."

"High Sierra is the name of our latest update," said the kid. "There is no Low Sierra." He handed back my computer. "Type in your username and password."

"Okay." I tapped away at my keypad. All of a sudden, a recipe for Duck a l'orange popped up. The page was frozen but visible.

"You like to cook duck?" asked the kid.

"I don't know. I never made it. My computer froze."

"Orange duck is delicious," he said licking his upper lip. "You should try it."

"Get rid of the beach balls, and I will."

Using the touchpad, the kid clicked around until he found something. "Here's your problem." He pointed to a status readout on my monitor. "Your processor is slow."

"That's not the only thing that's slow, Kid. Tell me something I don't know."

"I mean it. The High Sierra update sucks the life out of slow processors. Your computer is old. It can't handle it."

"I can relate. Now I'll never know how to prepare Duck a l'orange."

"Don't worry, Tracey with an 'e'." He patted me on the back. "I can tell you how to make it."

"How?"

"First thing you do is—shoot the duck."

Menopause

On a recent visit to my male gynecologist, we discussed menopause. Why? Because it is effing annoying, that's why.

"Dr. Don," I said, "the prefix for menopause is m-e-n, right?"

"Yes, Tracey, it is. What's your point?"

"My point is that that spells men. Menstruation begins with m-e-n, but men never get a period. Period! Mentorships begin with m-e-n but I know women mentors, too. Men-sa is not just for men."

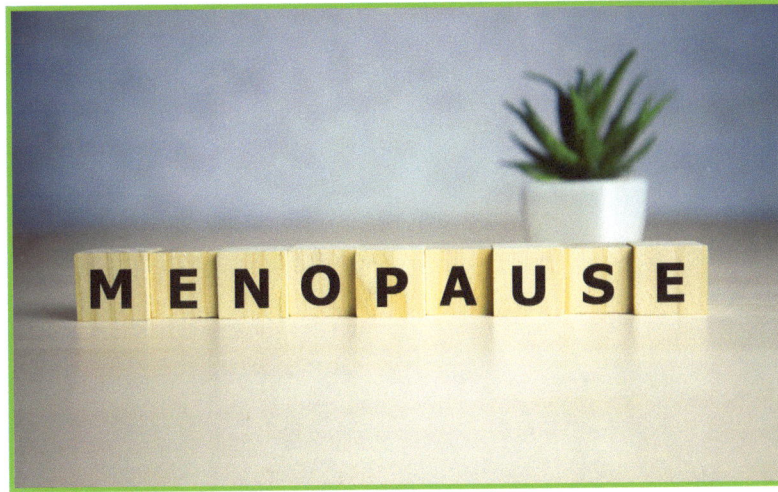

"I get it, Tracey," he interrupted my rant. "How can I help you?"

"Are you familiar with the phrase, if you can't stand the heat then get out of the oven?"

"Yes."

"Well, I can't stand the heat. I want to get out of the oven. It's time for men to carry the torch."

"It doesn't work that way."

"Well, it ain't working this way either, Doc."

"I hear you, Tracey," he nodded. "Those are just words."

"But words matter, don't they?"

"Yes, they do. But m-e-n is a prefix. What's really going on, Tracey?"

"Menopause is going on. I want it to go off. Can you pause it, please?"

"No, but I can treat it."

"Then treat it like it was inhabiting your body because it's menacing mine. In fact, it's a menu for disaster."

"Don't you mean, recipe for disaster?"

"See?" I argued. "I can't stop using m-e-n words. I'm a mental case."

"You'll be on the mend soon. I guarantee it."

"Outta the mouths of men," I sighed. "Thanks... I think."

"Don't MENtion it."

The Dress

My girlfriend Pam is the most stylish woman I know. I needed a fancy dress so I called her. "Pam," I said, "I have a wedding to go to at the Beverly Hills Hotel. Will you meet me at Saks and help me find something to wear?"

"Is it black tie?" she asked.

"Yes, and everyone going to this soiree has already seen me in my black silk palazzo pants and ivory satin top. I can't wear that outfit again. I'm desperate."

"Meet me upstairs at Saks on Tuesday," said Pam. "I'll have Olina help us."

On shopping day, I brought along Spanks, a fur shrug, a black clutch, and silk shoes. When I arrived, Pam was standing at the top of the escalator holding up a Lela Rose floral dress.

"Hi Pam," I said. "What's that?"

"Try it on, Tray, I'm getting a vibe from it." I put on the dress and modeled it for Pam and Olina.

"Oh, my God!" exclaimed Pam. "That's a 10. Isn't it a 10, Olina? It's totally a 10. You *have* to buy it."

"I think it's a 12," I said coyly.

"Not the size—the look. It's totally a 10." I stared at my image for a while. "You need different shoes. I'll go downstairs and get Rob to bring up some samples. What size are you?"

"Nine and a half. Low heel please, I have bad feet." Rob entered the scene with three boxes of shoes. I tried on pair #1.

"Try it on, Tray. I'm getting a vibe from it."

"Oh, my God!" bellowed Pam. "Those are a 10."

"You're right," said Rob. "I didn't have a nine and a half. How do they feel?"

"Good. I like the flower on the back." Pam, Olina, and Rob gawked at me in admiration.

"They're a 10," reiterated Pam. "For sure you *have* to buy them."

"What should I wear to cover my shoulders?" I asked the trio. "It could be a cold night."

"Show me the stuff you brought from home," said Pam. I showed her the fur shrug and black clutch.

"Oh, my God, NO!" she shrieked. "Those are all wrong. I'll go to the fur department and bring back some samples." Pam came back with Evelyn and Nancy, carrying piles of furs and handbags. I tried them on. Pam, Olina, Rob, Evelyn, and Nancy gawked at me... again. "I think you need the dress altered under the armpits," said Pam. "It's gaping a bit."

"I'll get our seamstress," said Stephen, the store manager, who was hovering nearby. Moments later, he came back with Ayako, and she pinned the underarms of the dress. Pam, Olina, Rob, Evelyn, Nancy, Stephen, and Ayako gawked at me.

"You'll need the right lipstick," said Pam. "Not too bright, not too nude. I'll go get Richard at the Bobbi Brown counter. He'll bring a few samples." Richard brought up a tray of lipsticks. I slathered on Pink Punch. "That's a 10 for sure. Don't you love the way you look, Tray? You *have* to buy that lipstick." Pam, Olina, Rob, Evelyn, Nancy, Stephen, Ayako, and Richard gawked at me.

"That's a 10 for sure. Don't you love the way you look, Tray?"

Ten days later, the dress was delivered to my house stuffed to billowy perfection. I hung it in my closet. On the day of the wedding, Jim and I drove from Rancho Mirage to Los Angeles. It took us about three hours. We pulled up to the valet at the 'W' Hotel at 3 p.m., and the wedding was set to begin promptly at 6. We couldn't afford to stay at the Beverly Hills Hotel after what I'd spent on the dress, shoes, fur, handbag, and lipstick.

We removed our suitcases and hanging bags from the car. The bellman loaded them onto the luggage cart. I carefully opened each garment bag. Now it was my turn to gawk.

Everything had made it to Los Angeles... except the dress.

Headache

Yesterday, I woke up with a headache, so I rummaged around our bathroom looking for meds but found none.

"Jim," I said, nudging him awake, "where are the headache meds?"

He tussled around a bit, then answered, "Check the spice cabinet in the kitchen for Tylenol."

That's strange, I thought, but okay. I dragged myself into the kitchen and opened the spice cabinet. On the rack between the cinnamon and cayenne were three bottles; Acetaminophen, Ibuprofen, and Naproxen.

"Geez," I said, confused by all the generic names. "Alexa, what is the generic name for Tylenol?"

The robot replied with a long explanation, "Here is something I found on Wikipedia, blah, blah, blah." I stopped listening after she said, 'Wikipedia.'"

I shuffled back into the bedroom. "Jim," I said, drooping my head. "What is the generic name for Tylenol?"

"I can't remember. Read the label."

"Can I borrow your glasses?"

"There's a pair in the kitchen," he advised. "I'm using these."

"Argh," I groaned, then pivoted out of the room. After locating a pair of reading glasses, I pulled out the acetaminophen, popped a couple in my mouth, and crawled back into bed.

An hour later, Jim nudged me awake. "Hey, Tray, want a homemade muffin?"

"Sure," I said, sitting up in bed. I took a bite. "Ew, this is disgusting." I spit it into a tissue. What spice did you put in these—because it's not cinnamon! Yuck!"

"I followed the All-Bran recipe," was his excuse. "But I didn't have my glasses on." He took a bite of a muffin. "Oh crap. I must have used cayenne."

Guess who has a headache now.

Father's Day

"Happy Father's Day, Jim," I said, adding a gentle kiss to his lips. We cuddled. "I love you, Jim. I love you for the life we've created. I love you for the children we've raised."

"Thank you, Tracey. I'll never tire of hearing those words."

"I bought you something," I said, getting out of bed. "I'll be back in a sec." I hopped out of bed and brought back a pretty wrapped box.

"Shoes?" he said smiling.

"How'd ya know?"

"The box," he said, eyeing the obvious shoe-box.

"Oh, right." So much for surprises.

Jim opened the box. "Allbirds," he said, as he held them and admired their softness, "I've always wanted a pair of these. Thank you." He flipped them over and noticed the white bottoms were a little dirty. "Someone's already worn these shoes, the soles are scuffed." Jim showed me the bottom of the shoes.

"I confess," I said, slouching a bit. "It was me."

"Why did you wear my new shoes?"

"You know the saying, you never really know a man until you've walked in his shoes?"

"Yes. I've heard that before."

"I wanted to test that hypothesis."

"C'mon, Tracey. What did you learn?"

"I learned that your shoes gave me room to grow, something you've always afforded me."

"Ah, that's sweet." He rubbed my arm.

"I learned your shoes offered security and protection, something I've always felt when you're around." Jim kissed my forehead.

"I learned that the shoes were warm, something you always are to me and the girls." I put my slender arms around Jim's strong shoulders and said, "Now I know what it's like to walk in your shoes."

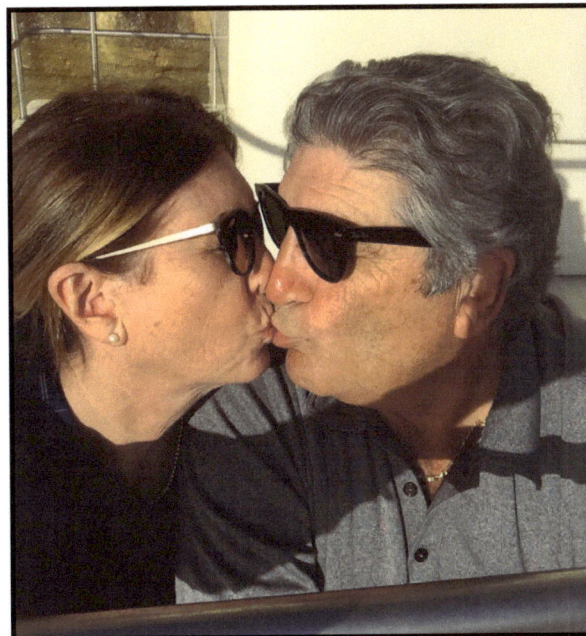

"Happy Father's Day, Jim. We make a great pair."

The Necklace

This is a tale about disappearing eyewear. Stay focused.

"Have you seen my glasses, Tracey?" asked Jim. "The red I Need You, readers?"

"Is I Need You the brand name?"

"Yes. I have three pairs."

"I thought all of our readers came from Costco."

"They don't," he said stridently. "The girls bought me red I Need Yous and I loved them so much that I went online and bought a couple more."

"What colors?"

"Black and blue. I've been hiding them."

"Why?"

"Because you take my glasses all the time and I can never find them when I need them."

"You should keep them on a chain around your neck. And anyway, I don't *take* them, I *borrow* them."

"I'm not wearing readers around my neck. My mother used to do that. Can you cut me some slack?"

Jim is such a nice guy, but he is always losing glasses. I knew where his I Need You's were. I always know where his glasses are, but this time I wouldn't tell him because I was making him something unforgettable. I felt a little guilty, but not for long. "Let's not argue, Honey. I'll look around. They'll show up."

I went to my home office to work on the necklace. Ten minutes later, Jim walked in. "Did you find my glasses?"

I slammed the lid on the craft box that housed his glasses. "No," I said innocently, as my heart jumped out of my chest. "I don't know where your glasses are, sorry."

Once he left, I lifted the lid and found three pairs of colorful I Need You readers, plus a silver chain and clasp.

Knock. Knock. Jim walked in again. "I ordered three pairs of I Need You's online, they're being overnighted."

"Great," I smiled. "What colors?"

"Grey, tortoiseshell, and silver. Why?" he asked.

"Because," I said, swinging my partially completed project. "I need six pairs of glasses to finish the necklace."

Snoring

I love my blue foam roller. She's my very own personal massage therapist. I use her after workouts or rounds of golf. But today, I needed her as soon as I woke up.

Getting on the blue foam roller looks like this. Stop. Drop. Plop. Rock. Roll. Balance. Inhale. Exhale. Sigh. This morning, however, I fell sound asleep on her. A half-hour later, I couldn't get up.

"Honey, will you give me a hand?"

"Where are you?"

"On the foam roller, my side of the bed. I can't get up."

"Oh jeez," he groaned. "Let me finish my Euchre game."

Meanwhile, I contemplated tipping myself over like a kayak. "C'mon Jim, I'm getting cold."

Finally, my husband stood over me. I reached for his arms, but he wouldn't lend a hand. "What if I weren't here?" He crossed his arms stubbornly.

"I guess I'd have to figure it out."

"Then, figure it out!" he demanded.

"You're such a pain in the ass," I said, staring up at him.

To be truthful, Jim was right to make me get up by myself. I work-out with a trainer, walk miles every day, play golf, cook meals, and write lots of funny stories. I sure as hell should be able to lift my body off of a foam roller. So, I took several deep breaths, wobbled side-to-side, raised my knees, secured my feet, lunged forward, and like a Pez emerging from its dispenser, I got up.

"You did it!" Jim praised. He winked at me. I slapped his ass.

"You should've helped me," I moaned. "I fell asleep on the damn thing because you kept me up all night."

"I did?"

"Yes, you did. By the way, did you know that humans breathe 22,000 breaths a day?"

"No."

"Well, they do. And as per my calculation, last night I had to endure 7,328 of your snores."

"How do you know that?"

"Figure it out!" I demanded.

Birds

I'll admit it. I talk to birds.

Phoebe, my favorite dove, was busy constructing a nest on an unstable branch directly outside of my office window. "Hey Phoebe," I said. "That branch is too flimsy. You may want to choose a sturdier location for your nest."

Days went by and Phoebe's building skills never improved. "Phoebe," I repeated, "that branch is a mistake. Where is Mortimer?" Mortimer is Phoebe's spouse. "Maybe he has a safer place for your chicks. Why don't you fly around and look for him?" Phoebe ignored me and kept working on her nest, but If she could tweet, I bet she'd say, 'Mortimer is a deadbeat dove. He doesn't help with anything. Gimme a break.'

Distracted and unable to write, I decided to google 'nesting materials for birds,' and found a solution. I tapped my office window. "Phoebe, the next delivery from Amazon is for you."

Coconut fibers, twine, and a cotton-tail ball arrived in a tidy little box. I carefully positioned each item beneath Phoebe's nesting tree.

"Phoebe, look at all the great stuff I bought for you. Use it to build a safer nest for your chicks."

"Who are you talking to?" asked Jim as he walked into my office.

"A dove named Phoebe. She's nesting outside my window. Look!"

"You're a riot, Tracey. There is a dove nesting outside of my office too, but I don't talk to him. I think you need help."

"No, I don't. Amazon to the rescue."

"Amazon? What did you buy from Amazon?"

"Nesting materials. Phoebe was struggling to find things for her nest so I bought her stuff on Amazon. Now she can build a gorgeous nest."

"Really? The bird outside of my office already built a really great nest."

"I bet it's Mortimer, Phoebe's husband. Let's go see!"

Jim and I went to have a look. "Mortimer," I said, "did you build this nest for Phoebe?" No tweet.

I rushed back to my window. Tap. Tap. Tap. "Phoebe, Mortimer is not a deadbeat dove—he's been building you a nest in the Palo Verde tree outside Jim's office." No tweet from Phoebe once again, but if she could tweet, I bet she'd say, 'he should have told me before I started this one. Jerk!'

While it is impossible to know which dove was which, if Phoebe and Mortimer were smart, they'd return every spring for more goodies from Amazon.

Washer/Dryer

My current Maytag washer and dryer have two settings, on and off. But the house rental I am living in has two brand new LG appliances perched atop pedestals.

"What the f*** are these?" I mumbled, facing the two behemoths. I opened the washing machine door. "Where do I load the detergent?"

I just went by instinct and threw in our white clothes with a Tide Pod that I brought from home.

What the hell does Smart Diagnosis mean?

Where's the start button? I wondered. The motherboard was digital, and I couldn't read what it said without glasses. So I touched everything, hoping to find a wash cycle. Nothing.

When I discovered a button that I believed to say, Start Disturbing, I pressed it, and something lit up. I'm used to hearing water fill the drum once the wash cycle begins, but I heard nothing. Finally, I gave up.

I walked to my desk across the hall from the laundry room and listened for sounds. When noises finally emerged, I began to write this story. About an hour later, I heard a Schubert jingle. The cycle was complete. I opened the washing machine door to remove our white clothes and pulled out a pair of pink cotton boxers. "Uh-Oh," I groaned. "Jim will be pissed."

I decided to take a closer look at that 'start' button so I found a pair of cheaters in a desk drawer. Turns out, the button didn't say, 'Start Disturbing,' it said, 'Smart Diagnosis.'

What the hell does Smart Diagnosis mean? If LG was so smart why didn't it tell me there was a pair of red undies stuck to the top of the drum?

Silver-lining... Jim looked great in his pink underwear.

Baseball

"Want to go see the Dodgers play the Padres, Tray?" asked Jim. "They're at Petco Park. We can take the train."

"Sure, I'd love to."

Sidebar: I like baseball, but, I kind of get distracted at games. Let me explain.

As soon as we walked through the turnstiles, I spotted a man with a badge. "Excuse me, Sir. Could you tell me where the Seaside Market is? I heard they have the best BBQ Tri-tip nachos."

"Oh, they do," he agreed. "Follow the ramp to the concourse level. You can't miss it."

"Thank you."

On our way to Seaside Market, something else popped into my head. "Hey Jim, do you think they have Vodka here?"

"I don't know. I've never been here."

"Over there," I said, pointing across the mall where I noticed a free-standing bar. "I'd like a Mai Tai, please," I said to the vendor."

"Are you 21?" he asked.

"No, but neither are my kids. They are 30 and 33." He filled a tall souvenir glass with pinkish liquid then garnished it with a pretty purple orchid. I thanked him and we moseyed along.

"Mai Tai's are made with Rum, not Vodka," Jim informed me.

"I like Rum too. Let's get our nachos then find our seats." We strolled past vendors until we found our gate. Sip. Sip. Munch.

"I love being behind home plate!" he marveled.

"Why are Santa Claus and tin soldiers on the field?" I asked.

"Because tonight's theme is Christmas in July."

"But it's 96 degrees outside."

"It's a theme, Tracey. That's all I know."

"Are you 21? No, but neither are my kids. They are 30 and 33."

By the end of the first inning, I had finished my nachos. By the end of the second inning, I had scrutinized every person sitting around me. I checked out their hair, tattoos, clothing, and food choices. I love to people watch.

"I'm going to get a hot dog," said Jim. " Want anything?"

"Maybe later."

Just as he left his seat, a roaming vendor walked up the aisle shouting, 'peanuts, churros, cotton candy, Cracker Jacks!' That tempted the crap out of me. Meanwhile, the guy next to me wearing a red antler headband shouted, 'peanuts!' The vendor tossed him a bag. I watched him crack open every single one, drooling. I decided to go to the washroom.

While waiting in line, all I could think of was wood-fired pizza. The next thing I knew, I had a slice in my hand and was walking back to my seat.

During the seventh inning, we stretched. "Want some dessert?" asked Jim.

"Yes, I want Cracker Jacks." The vendor tossed a box of the sweet treat and Jim caught it. "Hey, there's no prize in my Cracker Jacks."

"They stopped giving out prizes in 2016."

"How do you know that?"

"I don't know," he shrugged his shoulders. "I must have read it somewhere."

Jim is as smart as Alex Trebek. He knows a lot of trivia.

Endgame: Guess what I got in the bottom of the ninth inning?

Indigestion.

BTW – Dodger's won 3-2, but I couldn't tell you how.

Closing the Rental

Our two-month rental in Encinitas is over. This is what packing-it-up looked like on departure day.

"Hey, Jim," I said, "will you strip the bed and gather up the dirty towels while I go downstairs to tidy up the kitchen and family room?"

"Okay." He was engrossed in a Euchre game on his iPhone. "Should I start the wash or will housekeeping be doing it?"

"I'm not sure. I need to go downstairs and read the welcome book. I'll let you know."

Once downstairs, I flipped through the pages of the book but found no instructions on closing the house. "Wash them," I yelled up the stairway. "Towels too."

In the meantime, I ran the dishwasher, swept the floors, wiped down counters and sinks, cleaned out the fridge, and emptied all the trashcans.

Then, I went back upstairs to gather my suitcases and discovered a mound of dirty sheets and towels. "Why didn't you do the wash?" I asked.

"Because you told me not to," he said, packing his suitcase.

"No, I didn't. I told you to wash them, but

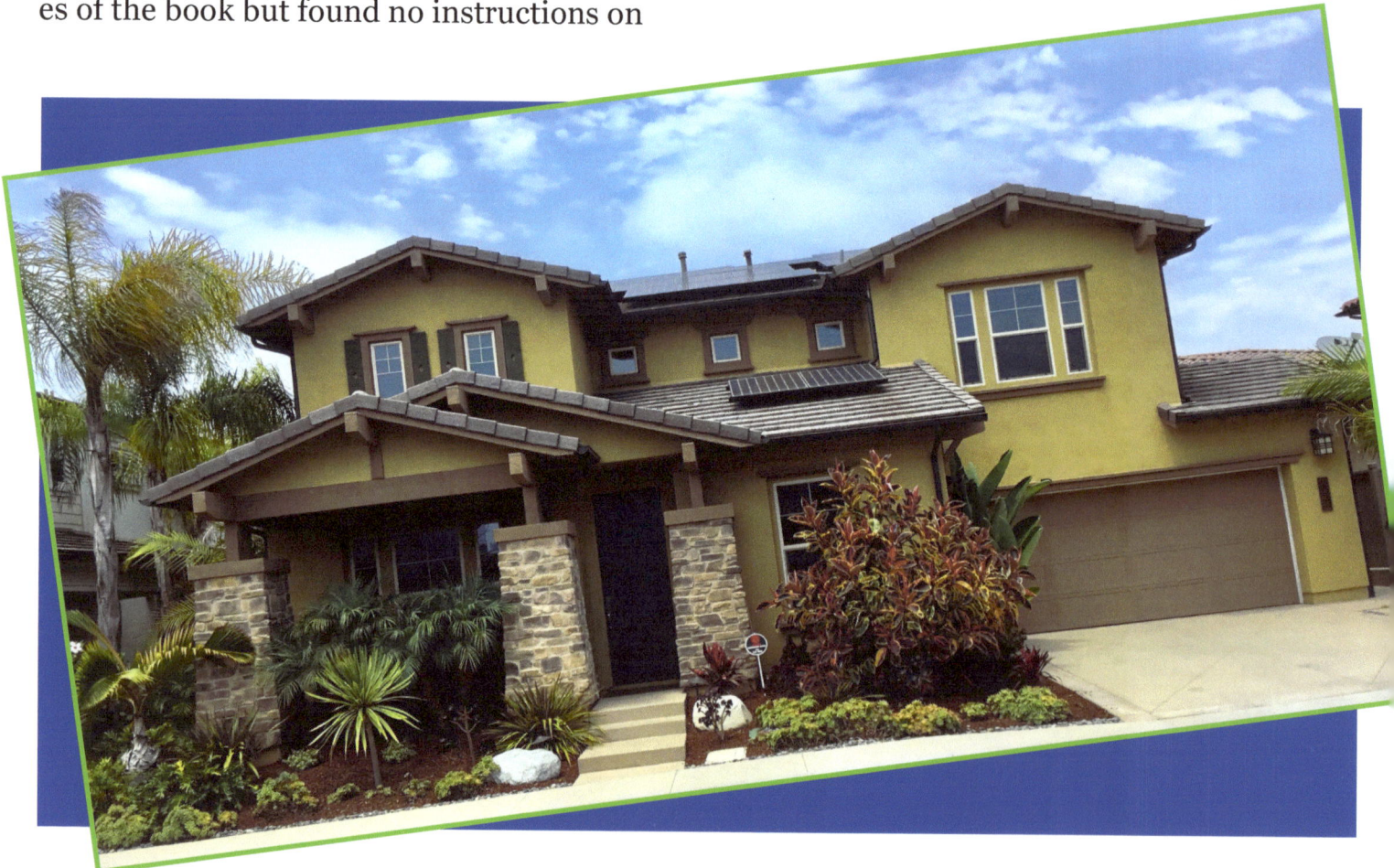

you were probably too busy playing euchre to listen."

"I heard you say, 'Don't wash them'."

"That's impossible, Jim."

"Should I wash them, now?" he offered.

"No, we don't have time. Checkout is at noon. I finished my chores, so I'm leaving."

"Did you get my camera, sandals, and my exercise bands?"

"Yes. Yes. And, yes." I kissed him goodbye and left the house.

Hours later, back in Rancho Mirage, I helped Jim unload his car. "What's this?" I said, holding up a king-sized pillow.

"My pillow."

"No, Jim, that's not your pillow. It's the owner's. I held up the pillow from his side of the bed and said, "This is your pillow." Just then, I received a text on my smartphone. I read it out loud.

> **"You were probably too busy playing Euchre to listen."**

Tracey, do you know where Gary's pillow is?

I shot him a dirty look.

Sorry Carol, I texted. Jim thought it was his. And, I'm sorry for not washing sheets and towels.

Her reply: No worries, I'll wash them. By the way, tell Jim he can keep the pillow, Gary snores too much on that one.

What a coincidence, I responded. Jim snores like an ape on it too.

Deciding What to Pack

In a few days, Jim and I would be river cruising down the Danube and visiting Prague, Vienna, and Budapest. It was time to pack. "Jim," I said, "did you know that rolling your clothes instead of folding them is a space-saver?"

"I'm folding mine, Tray."

"Why? Travel bloggers say rolling your clothes results in fewer wrinkles and provides extra room for your sized 13 shoes."

"I'll do it my way," he insisted. "You do it yours."

"Fine. Are you at least going to use the Eagle Creek packing organizers that Jason gave us?"

"Yeah, yeah," he said dismissively. "Give me a chance to lay out my clothes, will ya?"

In the meantime, I decided my entire wardrobe would consist of black, white, and beige garments. I'll mix and match, I thought. After carefully choosing each item, I was ready to roll. "I'm going to the garage to get suitcases, what size do you want?"

"I don't know. I'll get a suitcase when I'm ready."

"Fine." I headed to the garage. In under an hour, I had neatly packed my suitcase leaving room for my toiletries.

While I was in the bathroom pouring sunscreen into travel-sized containers, Jim yelled, "Come here, Tracey, I need you." When I re-entered the bedroom, I found Jim haunched over his suitcase.

"What's wrong?" I asked.

"Will you sit on my suitcase, please?"

"Oh Geez." I lowered my butt to the bag.

"Please don't criticize me. I know what I'm doing."

"Don't you think you overdid it?" I bounced up and down a few times.

"No. I weighed my suitcase."

"How?"

"I stood on the scale holding my suitcase. It weighs 48 pounds and British Airways allows 50 pounds."

"Isn't that cutting it kind of close, Jim?"

"I'm fine, Tracey. Enough."

Guess what we learned at the airport?

Jim had a vanity weight. It cost him $100.

Czech Your Manners

Before my trip abroad, I decided to learn how to say 'please' and 'thank you' in Czech. Here is how I prepared for my visit to Prague. "Siri?" I said, "how do you say 'please' in Czech?" Answer. "I can't translate into Czech yet, but I can translate into Spanish, Chinese, French, and a few others."

"But I'm not going to Spain, Mexico, China, or France," I said to my device, "I'm going to Prague." Since Siri was useless, I decided to google Czech 'please' and 'thank you' on my desktop. I discovered that the word 'please' is 'prosim' and 'thank you' is 'dekuji.' Without a clue as to how these words were pronounced, I decided to use sound-alikes that would be easy to remember. So on our trip, I will use *possum* for please and *jacuzzi* for thank you.

I decided to practice my newfound manners on Jim in the airport lounge before we boarded the plane. "Jim," I said politely, "can I have a power plug, *possum*? My phone is low on battery."

"Not now, Tracey. I'm reading an email about our taxes."

"But I need a power plug, *possum*."

At that very moment, a waitress arrived at our table and said, "Would you like a drink, Sir?"

Without hesitating, Jim looked up at her and said, "I'll have a Johnny Walker Black on the rocks."

"Ma'am?" she said, looking at me. "Would you like something to drink?"

"No *jacuzzi*. Maybe later."

"I'm sorry, Ma'am," she said. "Did you say you wanted something boozy?"

"Oh no, Miss. I'm learning to speak Czech."

"Okay," she said, rolling her eyes, "but I speak English. What would you like to drink?"

"I'll have a Tito's on the rocks with a couple of olives, *possum*."

Jim nudged me. "What's wrong with you, Tracey? You're being so rude."

"No, I'm not. I'm being polite."

"Can I get you anything else, Sir?" asked the waitress, turning her attention to Jim.

"No thank you," he said, smiling. "Just the check, please."

I turned to the pretty waitress and said, "*Jacuzzi*."

Tour Guide

Vera was a tour guide on our bus from Prague to Vilshofen, Germany. We were part of a convoy departing from the Hilton Hotel.

"Velcum effryvun," she said, standing in the aisle of the bus. "Vud you plees check for yur pazzports and make sure all yur valuables ver remooft from yur vroom safe. Ve dun't vant yur belonginks left behint. Ve vill zoon be trafflink on de highvay to Pilsner and I vil show you places along da vay."

The travelers who understood what she said, complied.

"Vel," said Vera, "virst, impotant bizzness. Ve hat batroom on bort bus, vel, it's against German vule to use it vile ve movink. So. Vel. Ve vil schtop in two-howass fa you to use. Or, vel, ve vil also schtop at very nice Courtyard by Marriott vare you can use batroom for vree."

I had a sudden urge to pee.

Vera's cell phone rang. She answered it, then alerted us to the news. "Vun minut, pleeze. I jus got vird dat our udder bus hass problem. Vel, they vill need to go back to da Hilton for anudder bus."

We were sad about the fate of our fellow travelers but thrilled with Vera, our astute tour guide.

"Vel," sighed Vera, concerned for the other bus. "I neets a vacashun. Ven I vinish here, I'm goink on holiday to America."

As we pulled into the port, Vera removed her headset and disembarked the bus. One by one passengers thanked her for her funny stories about her beloved homeland. Now it was my turn.

"Vera," I said, "where are you going in America?"

"I'm goink to take my daughta to Beverly Hilts," she answered.

"That's where I'm from," I said enthusiastically. "I would be happy to be your tour guide when you arrive."

"Dats a'nize," she said, shaking my hand. "Giff me yer numbah, I vil call you ven I arrive."

I wrote down my phone number then handed it to Vera.

Guess what she said?

"Dekuji."

"*Jacuzzi*," I said, recognizing the word. "That means thank you."

Vera's toothy smile conveyed, you're welcome.

Whose Default Is It?

I decided to write a story from the viewing deck of my river cruise wearing a bright white bikini while sipping a buttery chardonnay and admiring the Viennese countryside.

I opened Word then clicked on New Document. I typed 'I Don't Have Time for Green Bananas #29.'

"What the font!" I yelled, "I can't read a damn word." The toolbar read Calibri body 11pt. No matter what I typed, I couldn't read it. Sip. Sip.

"Siri, what is Calibri body?" Dumb question, so I'll blame it on the wine.

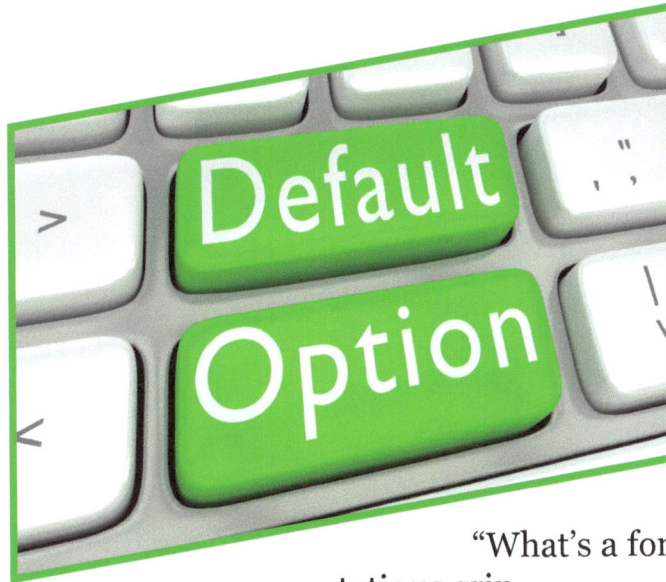

The answer, "Colibri Body is a natural anti-insect product."

"Okay, wrong. Bug-off." Next question, "Siri, how do I default to a new font and size?" The answer, "Transfer to a new computer." Sip. Sip.

"You're kidding right? This *is* a new computer."

A man in a nearby chaise lounge turned toward me and said, "Pardon?"

"Nein," I said, thinking he was German. Sip. Sip.

I didn't want to appear like a crazy woman who has conversations with her computer so I googled the same phrase and found seven trouble-shooting options. #7 was—Consider using a magnifier.

"Seriously?" I blurted. "C'mon!"

The man kept staring at me. "I speak English," he said with a German accent. "You need help?"

"I'm trying to change the font size in a word document." Sip. Sip.

"What's a font?" he said with a flirtatious grin.

OMG, he's a pervert! I was convinced.

Here's the point. I've earned a Master's degree and given birth twice, none of which were easy.

What I don't have are my Word Documents defaulted to Times New Roman, 14pt.

Whose default is it?

Answer: It's de-fault of de-wine. Sip. Sip.

I Do Declare

Jim decided early on that he was going to buy a watch in Vienna. I didn't want to buy anything because the declaration process is scary and intimidating. Jim disagreed, so he purchased a Pilot Watch by IWC.

"Cute watch," I said. "Now give me the receipt and I'll put it in my purse."

"No Tracey, I'll keep it in my wallet."

"Mr. & Mrs. Fuller, today is your lucky day."

Jim's wallet holds scraps of paper that fly away like feathers in a soft wind every time he retrieves a credit card.

We went to lunch. "I've got everything under control, Tracey," he said, sipping a Pinot Noir and inspecting the receipt.

After lunch, Jim was determined to buy me a watch for my birthday. We strolled the cobblestone streets and came to a heavy gilded gold door with a side doorbell. "Let's go in there," I said, eyeing a Cartier-style watch. An armed guard buzzed us in.

"That's a gorgeous watch. I'd like to try it on."

Our salesman lifted the dome and placed the Jaeger-LeCoultre Reverso watch on my wrist. "This watch was developed for polo players," he said, "to tuck away the fragile dial-side during play." I held it out for Jim to admire. "Isn't it gorgeous?" I said. Then Jim asked the salesman how much?

"Well, Tray, if you love it, you can have it."

"Really?"

"Yes. Happy Birthday."

"Do we have to declare it?" I asked admiring my new watch. "It'll cost a ton."

"Yes. We will declare it. It's no big deal. The exchange rate is good. I'll take care of it."

On the plane from Heathrow to Phoenix, Jim filled out the declaration forms. When we approached the Customs officer, my heart was racing.

"Show the agent your watch, Tracey." Jim held our passports and declaration papers as we stood in line.

"May I see your passports and your declaration form please?" said the officer. "How long were you traveling? What was the purpose of your trip? Did you purchase anything?" We answered then showed him our watches. "Do you have receipts?"

"Yes," said Jim, "I do." He really did. Phew!

"Come with me please," instructed the agent. He escorted us to a nearby windowless room.

"Wait here until they call your name."

"Jim," I whispered, "this was a bad idea. It's going to cost a bloody fortune."

"Relax, Tracey. Don't worry."

"Easy for you to say," I snapped.

"Fuller," said the agent. We approached the counter and answered questions. He calculated the tax we owed on a scratch pad with a pencil. I was suspicious. "Your tax obligation is $350," he concluded. Jim promptly handed him a credit card.

"I'll be right back, Mr. & Mrs. Fuller," said the agent as he left us alone in the room. I was a ball of nerves so I chewed some gum and scowled at Jim a lot.

Ten minutes later, the agent re-entered the room. "Mr. and Mrs. Fuller," he said, "today is your lucky day. Our credit card processor is down. You will not have to pay any tax. Thank you for being honest and declaring your purchases."

"Really?" I said, throwing up my arms.

"Really," replied the agent.

"Shouldn't confetti drop from the ceiling now?" I looked up.

"Mrs. Fuller," said the agent, "this isn't America's Got Talent."

"Well, I do declare," I said, smiling at the uniformed officer. "It sure feels like it is."

TSA Pre ✓

Getting TSA Pre✓ for our trip to Prague was like winning the lotto, or so we thought. Then we discovered that TSA stands for Tough-Shit-Asshole.

We flew from Palm Springs to San Francisco. Here's what happened at SFO.

"Sir," said Mr. TSA to Jim, "are your pockets emptied?"

"Yes," said Jim with confidence as he walked through the archway.

Buzz. Buzz. "Back up, Sir," demanded the agent. "Remove your belt." Jim placed his belt in a small grey container. "Okay, Sir. You may walk through now." No buzz.

"Ma'am," said Mr. TSA, as I stood ready to walk in behind Jim. "You've been randomly chosen to be screened by our agent. Step aside."

I did as I was told. I stood in a glass cage on the designated footprints. "Hold for three seconds, Ma'am," she said. "You may exit now. Stand over there." Ms. TSA swirled a wand around my body. "Arms out," she ordered. "Spread your legs. Turn around."

From London to Prague, we were also TSA Pre✓. Once again, we were targeted for inspection. Back in the glass dome.

On our way home from Budapest to London, we were TSA Pre✓ approved. This time though, we were wearing brand new watches. Buzzzzzz.

At our boarding gate in London, Jim was wearing sunglasses because his eyes were sensitive from having a bad head cold. "Sir," said Mr. TSA to Jim. "Step aside. You have been randomly selected to be screened by our agent."

We finally made it to Phoenix, where we were required to go through Customs. This time though, we were *not* approved for TSA Pre✓ and the tough shits simply waved us through. Go figure.

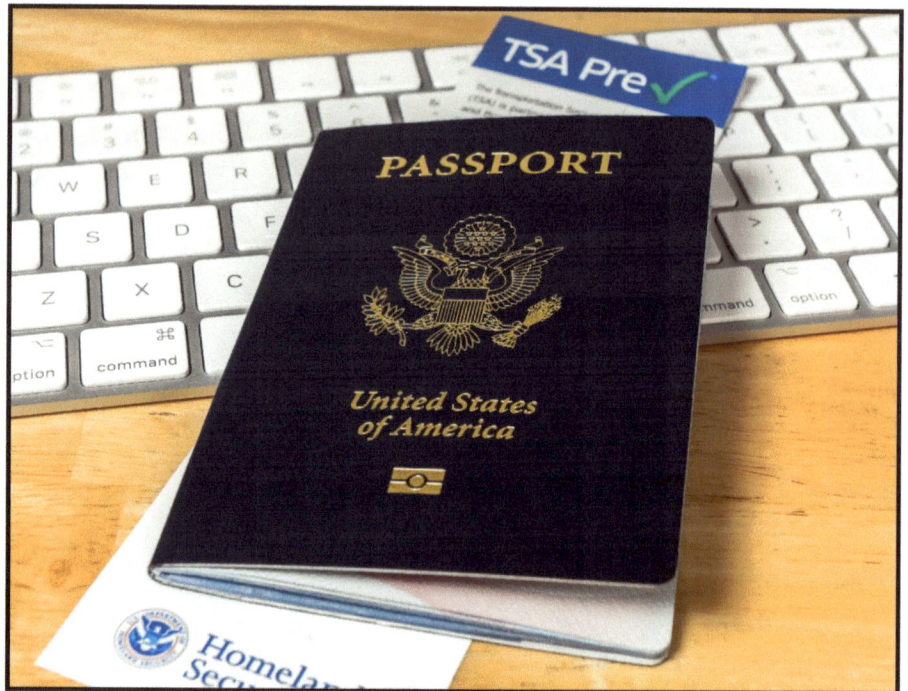

Sixth Sensor

On five different occasions, I discovered a sensor attached to a garment once I brought it home. The obvious question is, why didn't the alarm go off when I left the store? Sensors cannot be removed, by the way. I've tried and torn the fabric. Anyway, every time I found one, I had to go back to the store and risk being labeled a thief. What a nightmare! Here is one of my imagined scenarios:

I enter Neiman Marcus with the garment tucked away in a shopping bag, and as I walk through the front door I set off the store alarm. Buzz. Buzz. Buzz.

Two sales associates immediately pull me into an alcove in the designer shoe department. Customers trying on Louboutin shoes stare at me. Embarrassed and mortified, I turn my gaze away. Others are seen whispering to their friends.

One associate says sternly, "May I look in your bag, please?" I say, "I bought it the other day and the salesperson forgot to remove the sensor. I have the receipt!"

"Sure you do, lady," says one of the mean girls. "Come with me."

They each grab an elbow and drag me up the stairs to a third-floor corporate office. I'm told to sit in an interrogation room and await the general manager. My pulse is racing. I plead with them to believe me as the door slams shut, and I'm left staring at blank walls.

Soon thereafter, a woman resembling Cruella De Vil struts in and says, "Well now, what have we here?" Her expression is sinister, her voice loud and accusatory. At this point, I am jarred awake and covered in sweat.

Nightmare ends.

In lieu of past shopping experiences, I decided to buy a dress online. As I was packing for my trip to Prague, a gorgeous Camilla long-sleeve kimono maxi dress arrived on my doorstep.

I opened the box, peeked inside, and without trying it on packed the perfectly folded garment into my suitcase. On the night of our riverboat welcome reception, I unwrapped the beautiful dress and put it on.

Guess what I found dangling from the hem? The sixth sensor.

This one, thank God, was removable but carried a printed warning: 'Once this sensor is removed the dress is not returnable.'

Delicately, I detached the sensor from the hem, twirled around a few times expressing my sensor-free elation, then escorted my handsome husband to the sun-deck of our ship. Wunderbar!

You Work the Pedals and I'll Steer

Jim and I argue on road trips. Why? Because we're trapped in a car for hours and we've been married for 35 years. On this particular trip, we drove from Los Angeles to Tiburon, then on to Sonoma.

"Jim, why do you always pick the slowest lane?"

"Stop, Tracey! You always do this when I drive. Can't you stop?"

"But you miss off-ramps because you drive behind the slowest eighteen-wheelers. I'd like to arrive in Sonoma by sunset."

"We'll get there. Relax."

Jim follows trucks like zebras follow wildebeests in a migration. I think he suffers from trucker-trance. It's those sexy mudflap girls. I'm sure of it.

One more irritating Jim habit—he pumps the gas pedal. Lurch. Glide. Lurch. Glide. Lurch. Glide.

"Pass the truck already," I urged, "and stop pumping the gas pedal. I'm gonna barf."

"Here's an idea, Tray," Jim snarled. "You work the pedals and I'll steer."

"Seriously. I think you suffer from trucker-trance."

"What's that?"

"It's someone who mindlessly follows trucks outfitted with mudflap girls."

"I do not!"

I changed the subject. "Hey Jim, there's the town of Tracy, let's check it out. I'll drive from there." He pulled off the highway so that I could get a picture of the Tracy sign.

"See the lady on the horse next to the Tracy sign?" said Jim.

"Yeah, what about her?"

"She's your ride to Sonoma," he joked. "Your Uber Horse awaits."

"Very funny, Mister." I chose not to pester him for the remainder of the trip, but that's only because I was driving.

When we arrived at Gloria Ferrer Caves and Vineyards, we took a table on the terrace, popped open a bottle of bubbly, and toasted our arrival, just in time to see the sunset.

Rush & Choke

Yom Kippur is the Jewish holiday when you atone for your sins by fasting from sundown to sundown. If you succeed, then God clears your sin-slate for the New Year. Once the fast is over, you can sin again. Isn't life great?

This year, on the eve of our fast, we stopped at a roadside cafe in Oakland and feasted on fried chicken, waffles, gumbo, and beignets. The following morning, we had an 11 a.m. flight to Los Angeles for our break-the-fast festivities at my Auntie Mame and Uncle David's.

"Tracey," said Jim "are you really serious about fasting this year?" He sounded so forlorn.

"Honey, let's get some bacon."

"Are you listening to me?" said Jim, "I know you'll want a snack on the plane."

"I'll worry about tomorrow, tomorrow. In the meantime, finish your beer and we'll take a long walk." Burp. "I'm done." I folded my napkin. Cough. Cough.

"Sure," said Jim, "but you still haven't answered my question."

"What question?"

"Are you planning to fast tomorrow?" he repeated.

"Of course I am. I ate like a pig. I need to atone."

We drove home and went to bed. "Oh, my God!" I whimpered. "Why did I eat so much?"

"I told you, Tracey, you do this every year. You eat too much the night before a fast and then you feel like shit." I rolled away from Jim and eventually fell asleep.

Once I took my seat on the airplane, I opened the shade. Directly beneath my window was a conveyor belt loading snacks up to the galley. "Cheez-Its, stroopwafel, yummy," I mumbled. Jim overheard me talking about food.

"Does that mean you're not gonna fast, Tray?" I know he was hoping for a 'yes.'

"No. I just want what I can't have."

The plane backed away from the gate. The pilot made an announcement. "On behalf of Delta Airlines, I'd like to welcome you aboard flight 5742, service from Oakland to Los Angeles. This is your captain Ryan Rush, and next to me is your co-pilot Charlie Choke."

"Jim, can you believe that Rush and Choke are flying this plane? It sounds more like my eating habits before a fast."

"I told you, Tracey."

Good Yuntif.

Hats

Jim has a big head. I have a small head. Jim looks good in hats (when they fit). I look bad (no matter how they fit).

It was a sparkling sunlit day on Angel Island, so we decided to ferry over and spend a glorious afternoon touring around. We made a picnic lunch and grabbed a couple of hats.

"Please don't wear that hat, Jim," I begged. "It's too small and you know it. Wear your Smoky the Bear cap, it's perfect for hiking in the woods."

"I'm fine." He walked out of the house wearing his Panama hat. I grabbed my straw hat and we got into our car.

"Hold on." I reopened the car door, "I forgot sunscreen. I'll be right back." I ran into the house and grabbed Jim's Smoky the Bear cap.

Noticing that I was holding his cap, Jim said, "That's not sunscreen."

I defended my action. "I don't want a picture of you in that goofy hat. It was Debbie's, remember? She let you borrow it in Newport because you needed it. When she offered for you to keep it, you should've said no."

"I like it, Tracey. It fits fine. Stop."

Notice how Jim always says, 'stop.' I don't like it, so I kept going.

"Listen," I said, buttering him up. "You're a handsome guy. Will you at least take off the hat for pictures?"

"I don't know."

When we disembarked the ferry, we picked up a map of the island. "Let's take the Perimeter Trail to Camp Reynolds," I suggested.

"Okay."

At the crest of a hill, I called out, "Wow! this is the spot. You can see all the way to the Golden Gate Bridge." We stood at the cliff's edge admiring the view. "Now we need someone to take our picture." Finally, a young man shuffled up behind us.

"Excuse me," I said, holding out my iPhone, "will you take our picture, please?" The young hiker agreed and I handed him my device.

"No hats or glasses, Jim."

We wrestled a little. He removed his glasses.

"Now the hat, Babe. Take off the hat."

"No, Tracey. I'm going to wear it. Stop nagging me."

"Excuse me," said the hiker, observing our little tiff. "Sorry folks, but I need to catch up with my buddies. I think you'll have a few good ones to choose from."

On the ferry back to Tiburon, a gust of wind sent Jim's too-small Panama hat flying off his head and into Richardson Bay where it calmly floated away on a white-capped wave.

What a fitting end to our saga on Angel Island.

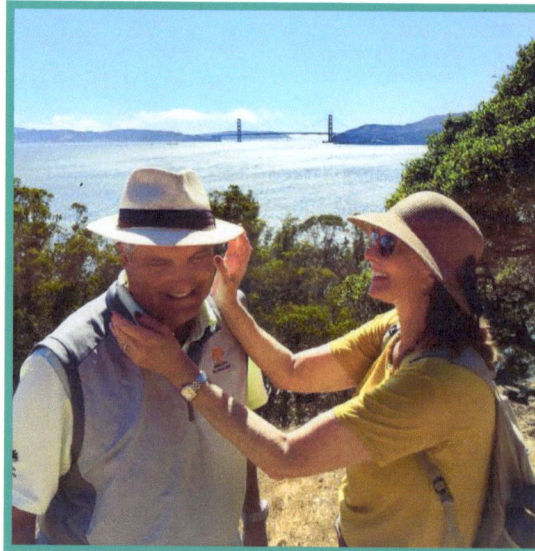

Telescope

Our Tiburon rental was outfitted with a Swarovski 65-HD telescope situated in a prime position for viewing Belvedere Island, the Golden Gate Bridge, and the San Francisco skyline.

While I was preparing dinner one night, Jim was happily glued to the telescope's eyepiece.

"What are you looking at, Jim?"

"I'm watching a couple eat dinner across the bay. I think we have the same candlesticks. You gotta check this out."

"Can you see what they are eating?"

"Yes. Salmon with Dijon and dill."

"You're kidding me, right? You can see that much detail?"

"Yes, and rice pilaf and asparagus."

"C'mon, let me see," I said, grabbing the eyepiece. I scanned the room. He was spot on about the meal but not the candlesticks. "Hey, they have that famous nude of John and Yoko. Speaking of nudes, I wonder if they watch us. I walk around here naked oblivious that someone over there might be a peeping Tom."

"I doubt it, Tracey. You can keep walking around naked, it's fine with me."

"I bet it is, Tom," I jested. "Should we close the shades?"

"No way. Let 'em watch."

The next day we heard jets soaring over our house. It was Fleet Week in San Francisco and the Blue Angels were performing an airshow. While peering through the telescope I watched two jets arc together. They formed a giant heart in the pristine blue sky directly over the Golden Gate Bridge.

"C'mere, Tracey." Jim pointed toward the sky. "That's why we have a telescope."

After looking through the Swarovski lens, we stepped onto the deck and admired the beautiful sight.

"I love you, T." He wrapped his arm around my shoulder.

"I love you too. What a beautiful view."

Football

"Hey, Tray," said Jim. "Do you want to go to a Bears/Bruins game at Cal Memorial Stadium this afternoon?"

"Sure, if I can figure out what to wear. It gets freezing by the water at night."

He hustled up some tickets while I shoved a bunch of warm clothes into my Adidas backpack.

Jim stopped me. "No backpacks—the ticket says no backpacks."

"Shoot, okay. I'll take my large yellow Longchamp purse. That'll hold our jackets." I shuffled stuff around and we hurried out the door.

"I can't wait to eat lunch at the stadium before game time." Jim got into the car. "Texas BBQ and a beer would taste really good right now."

"Do you think they'll have anything I can eat? I can't eat junk. I'm on the Gundry diet, ya know."

"I don't know. You'll find something."

Just in case, I ran back into the house and grabbed walnuts, a banana, and a dark chocolate bar with macadamia nuts. We headed over the Richmond Bridge and found a place to park in a nearby church parking lot. As we began to stroll toward the stadium, Jim noticed that most of the women around us were carrying clear plastic shoulder bags instead of purses.

"Excuse me," I said to a lady wearing blue and gold striped shoes, "are purses like mine allowed into the stadium?"

"No," she said, "only a small clutch or a see-through bag."

> *"Let's crash that party. You can get your Texas BBQ and beer, and I'll eat my pocket picnic."*

"Shit, Jim. What am I gonna do?"

"We gotta go back to the car and put your purse in the trunk. It's no big deal."

"It is a big deal," I argued. "I have a purse full of winter clothes in here. I can't leave them in the car. We'll freeze tonight."

"You have to, or they won't let you in."

We walked back to the church parking lot where I agonized over how to carry all my shit. In the meantime, Jim began a cheer, "Gimme a C! Gimme an A! Gimme an L!"

"Very funny, Shithead," I stuffed our pockets with everything that would fit. "Gimme a break!"

Once inside the stadium, we walked past a grassy knoll overlooking the shimmering bay. It looked like a private party was going on and I wanted in.

"Let's crash that party," I said. "You can get your Texas BBQ and beer, and I'll eat my pocket picnic."

I persuaded Jim to follow me to the check-in booth where a young man was verifying ID's as he guarded the entrance. "Are you with the baseball group?" he asked.

I thought that was a strange question considering we were at a football game, but without missing a beat I said, "Yes we are."

Oops. My bad.

He ushered us in.

"You just crashed a private party, Tracey." We wandered around looking for a table.

"I know," I grinned. "Let's eat."

After grabbing food and a couple of drinks, we sat down next to a very pretty squad of uniformed women carrying pompoms.

"Hey ladies," I said. "Will you take a picture with my husband?"

"Of course," they all replied kindly.

I instructed Jim to stand in the middle of the beautiful cheerleaders, then before I took the picture I shouted, "Gimme a J! Gimme an I! Gimme an M!"

Everyone had a smile on their face, but none as bright as Jim's.

The Bruins beat the Bears 37 to 7. Cheers!

Yacht

The sky was an unspoiled blue. The bay beckoned. About fifty yards away from where we were dining in Sausalito, three sexy yachts urged us to pay a visit. A blue and white 'for sale' sign was visible on the port side of the vessels. A gunmetal grey and white forty-two-foot cruiser attracted us (me) the most. After we dined, we climbed aboard.

"Wow, Jim," I said. "This is sexy."

"We're just looking, Tracey. Don't start."

We took off our shoes and stepped onto the polished vessel. I sat on a pearl white pleather bench, draped my arms dreamily over the backrest, and said, "Let's sell our house and live on this!"

"Stop, Tray." Jim entered the cabin.

"I'm serious. We could totally live on this yacht. It'd be so fun." Jim leisurely took a seat in the captain's chair and lowered the armrest. I walked through the galley and eyed two spectacular staterooms. "You've got to see this," I said. "The master bedroom has an upholstered headboard, a skylight, and a mounted flat-screen TV."

I bounced on the bed testing its springiness. "Come here, Jim, check it out."

"I'm busy, Tray. Stop."

I smoothed out the quilted bedspread then opened the ensuite bathroom door. Whoa, I thought. This bathroom is big. There are six feet of headroom in the shower. "You wouldn't have to duck your head. You'll love it!"

"We're just looking, Tracey."

"I know. But let's find out how much it is."

As Jim was chiding me, a woman came aboard. Her name was Trish. "Hello," she said kindly. "Are you thinking about buying a yacht?"

"Yes," I said in rapid response before Jim could say, 'No, just looking.'

I was serious. I've always loved boating. When I was nine-years-old, my dad loaned our boat to his insurance agent, and the guy crashed it. After the incident, my dad decided not to replace the boat. I was really upset about the loss, and I have never given up on the dream of having another boat someday.

"Would you like something to drink?" asked Trish. "Wine, water?"

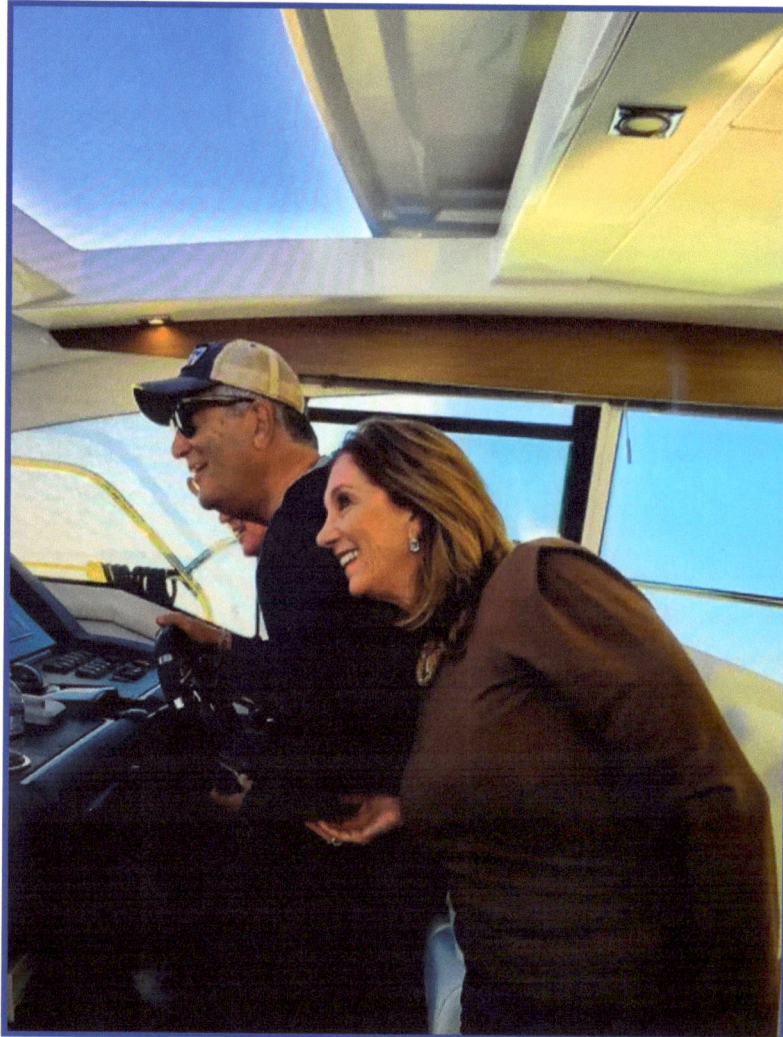

"Wine would be nice, thank you." Jim shot me a dubious glance. I didn't care. I was checking out my new digs and wine was being poured.

Trish explained to Jim how the yacht was outfitted with a joystick that enabled the vessel to pull away from a dock sideways. She gave him a brief tutorial on horsepower and ease of operation. All the while, I opened kitchen cabinets, peered into closets, and luxuriated on cushions at the bow. Heaven.

Trish followed me to the front of the yacht where there were two chaise lounges. "Ah, the good life. Join me." I offered Trish the lounge next to me. We held up our drinks for a toast. "To a Fuller yacht life," I said, tapping her glass.

"I like the sound of that," said Trish.

"So do I."

"Would you like to demo it, Tracey?" she asked.

"Hell yeah, I would!"

"Okay, when?" I thought about our week of activities. It occurred to me that our friends Hunt and Debbie were coming to visit us on Thursday. Then I thought hey, maybe they'll want to partner with us on the yacht. After all, they like boats, too.

"How about Thursday afternoon around 3:30," I said, after checking my iPhone calendar. "Can we take a three-hour-tour like on Gilligan's Island?"

Trish laughed. "Maybe. Here's my card."

I confirmed the demo ride with Trish via email and the four of us met her on the yacht. Her colleague George came aboard shortly thereafter.

With a swivel of the joystick, our crew of six pulled away from the dock and into the magnificent San Francisco Bay. "Champagne anyone?" said Trish, pulling a bottle of Mumm Napa Brut from the fridge.

"You bet," I said, pinching myself.

Debbie and I secured our hats as we glammed-out on the stern of the boat. Hunt and Jim stood beside George and watched how he operated the vessel. Soon thereafter, Jim took the helm and captained the ship.

Minutes later, tracking our speed at twenty-five knots, our sexy grey yacht was hydroplaning and heading straight for the golden gates. We idled slowly as we passed beneath the iconic structure. "C'mon," I said, bending backward to admire the expanse of the bridge. "This is breathtaking."

Trish orchestrated a photo of all four of us framed in by the deep orange structure then asked if we wanted to go to Sam's Anchor Café in Tiburon for a cocktail and their famous truffle fries. "Absolutely," I said without hesitation. Jim didn't say a word.

The six of us cruised across the bay, docked the boat at Sam's then took a patio table looking out at our (my) new yacht. Trish raised her pomegranate Mojito high into the air and said, "To Thurston, Lovey, Professor, and Mary Ann on their brand-new SS Minnow." We clanked our rims and sipped the dream. Our three-hour-tour ended when Captain Jim manhandled the joystick and docked us safely in Sausalito where our journey had begun.

"Whaddaya think Thurston Howell the Third?" I asked my handsome husband.

"Lovey," he said, "I think it's marrrrrvelous."

Dog

It was six a.m. in Tiburon, CA., a beautiful peninsula reaching into the San Francisco Bay. Our rental home provided a magnificent view of Belvedere Island, Sausalito, and the entire San Francisco skyline. For days, we awoke to windblown oak trees and swirling whitecaps.

Then one morning in late October, a smoky whiteness clung to our sliding glass doors as moss clings to a rock, and that changed everything.

"Jim," I said, gently nudging his shoulder, "wake up! We're blanketed with fog."

"I'm sleeping. Don't wake me up."

"But it's so cool. You can't see the bay. In fact, you can't even see the patio furniture. It's like being inside a snow globe that's just been shaken."

"Leave me alone." So, I left him alone in bed and roamed around the house.

Our house was 60% windows, the optimal design choice for an area such as this. The eeriness of looking outside our kitchen window and seeing nothing but white-dampness was strange. After all, we are desert dwellers, and at home fog is nonexistent.

By 7:30 a.m., I heard Jim shout from the bedroom, "Tray, where are you? We're totally fogged in."

"You're kidding me, right?" I watched my shirtless husband stroll toward the kitchen.

"I tried to wake you up an hour ago but you blew me off. I'm glad you finally got to see the fog. Want some breakfast?"

"Sure. Do I have time to take a shower first?"

"Of course. I'll wait until you get out."

> Her white-rimmed eyes stared at me while I held a colander of spinach.

I puttered around the kitchen rinsing spinach and slicing tomatoes when suddenly the fog began to lift, revealing a unique backyard visitor.

I stood very still. Her white-rimmed eyes stared at me while I held a colander of spinach. If she could talk I bet she'd say, 'Gimme some of that!'

I named her Dog, a combination of deer and fog, and decided to engage her in a short conversation. "Dog," I said, peering out of the window, "want some breakfast?"

Jim emerged from the bathroom. He overheard me talking to Dog.

"Who are you inviting to breakfast?"

"A deer named Dog," I said matter-of-factly.

"Who?" he sounded confused.

"A deer named Dog. She's in our backyard and I'm going to give her your breakfast. What took you so long in the shower?"

"I needed to shave," he said, shrugging his shoulders."

Jim's eggs were rapidly cooling while resting on a tall mound of spinach surrounded by plump heirloom tomatoes.

"You're a riot," he said, as he slid back his chair.

"I'm serious. I'm planning to feed Dog some spinach. I fell in love with her while you were in the shower."

"I don't advise you do that. Deer are experts at finding their own food."

"But she really liked watching me prepare breakfast. To her, it was like watching the Deer Food Network. She wanted to taste it."

"No," he insisted. "She didn't."

After breakfast, when Jim left the kitchen and Dog wandered aimlessly from our backyard, I sprinkled a few spinach leaves at the base of our pretty Japanese maple.

I'll be sad if I never see Dog again. But fog, not-so-much.

Fowl

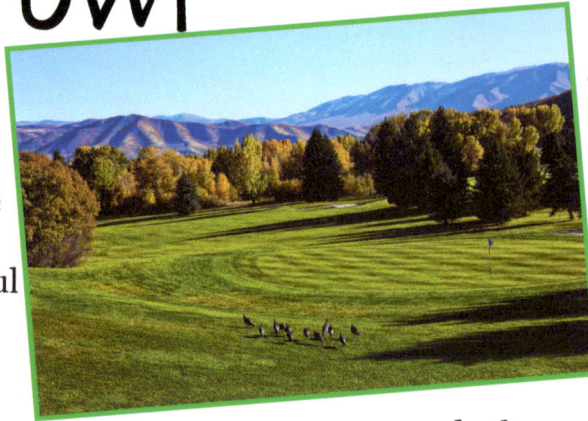

Before departing Tiburon to drive to Rancho Mirage, we thought it wise to take our car in for an oil change and tire rotation. I suggested that we golf while the car is being serviced. Jim agreed. But something went afoul in executing the plan. "We'll take the car to Petaluma," I said, "and play a course nearby. I can't remember the name, but I know there was some type of fowl in the name like Duck Links."

"Duck Links?" said Jim. "You're hysterical. I think you mean Rooster Run."

"That's it! Let's play there. When you call the Cadillac dealership, ask for a loaner, please."

Jim devised a plan. "We're all set. We'll drop off the car at 9:30 and play Rooster Run at 11."

"Great!"

We arrived at Victory Cadillac in Petaluma and picked up our loaner vehicle. "Mr. Fuller," said our sales technician, "I overheard you talking about playing golf at Rooster Run but I believe they're closed. Give me a second and I'll call for you."

"That's okay," said Jim. "I made a tee-time online. It's no problem."

We thanked the young man, drove to Rooster Run and while Jim dealt with our clubs, I went into the pro shop to check us in. "Fuller," I said to the starter. "We have an eleven o'clock tee-time."

"I'm sorry," he said. "I don't have a tee-time for Fuller. Could it be under another name?"

"Jim or Tracey. My husband made the tee-time online."

Jim walked in the pro shop only to hear the bad news. "I'm sorry," said the starter, "but I can't find your reservation. Why don't you check your email?"

Jim was pissed. He checked his email. "Oh shit, Tracey. Our tee-time is at Foxtail."

"Foxtail?" I said, bug-eyed. "That's not a type of fowl."

"I messed up, Tray. You got me thinking about animals and it confused me."

"You really cocked this one up, Mister."

"Sorry," said Jim. "If we hurry, we can make it to Foxtail. Let's go."

We said our goodbyes to the starter at Rooster Run then headed North to Rohnert Park. Unfortunately, Foxtail was closed. A sign was posted in front that read, "We apologize for the inconvenience, but due to our latest re-seeding, the course has been overrun by wild turkeys."

I call that fowl play.

Turkey

Kishka is a Yiddish word meaning guts. The following is a sentence using the word 'kishka.'

I eat my kishkas out every year during the holidays.

Why do I eat my kishkas out? Because the holidays are stressful. Let's begin with Thanksgiving since it is only days away.

I went to Trader Joe's and bought a 'kosher' turkey. Kosher turkeys are kishka-free. No giblets, thanks God. But I still felt like I needed to give the bird a bath before rubbing its skin with fresh herbs. So, I removed the plastic wrap, drained the bloody juices, and submerged the bird in cold water. I talked to the turkey while the task was underway. This is what I said.

"You're so f***ing heavy!" I complained while carrying the bird to the sink. "Lighten-up, would you please?"

No answer.

At that point, I named my turkey, Heavy. (Remember, I talk to birds).

"Have a good soak, Heavy," I said, while gingerly placing him in a sink filled with cold water. "I'm going to prepare your herbs."

While plucking Thyme one sprig at a time, I boogied to my favorite song, Uptown Funk. Thyme is such a nuisance. Rosemary and Sage are user-friendlier. Good tunes make the task much more pleasant.

I lifted Heavy out of the sink, dried him off, then massaged him with herbed butter. He felt so smooth. "You doin' ok?" I asked. "Don't take this personally, Heavy, but I have to tie you up now."

I retrieved some string, then tucked his wings beneath him. Next, I wrapped twine around his wings, crossed his legs, and tied them together, too. "Sorry, Heavy."

After the bondage exercise, I decided to take a stroll to unwind in my courtyard. Perched on a mound of sand-colored pebbles, adjacent to a tall ocotillo plant, sat a rusty metal turkey sculpture we inherited from my mother-in-law. Why? I'll never know. Anyway, his rusty eyes glared at me as I walked by.

"Don't gimme that look," I said pointedly. "You should be thankful. No one's ever going to eat YOU."

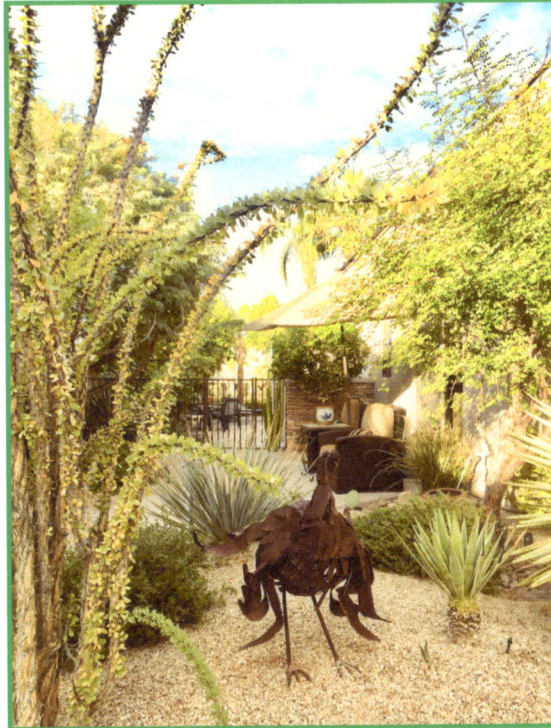

Ceiling

Crash! Bang! Boom!

"What the hell was that?" I said to Jim as we entered our home in Rancho Mirage after being away for months.

"I don't know. Move!" He shoved me aside and ran into the living room.

"Uh oh!" he said, "the ceiling collapsed in our dining room." Water rained down from a four-foot hole, soaking our antique credenza and narrowly missing a family portrait that hung above it.

"Holy shit! What are we going to do?"

"Go get a bucket. I'll take down the painting."

The bucket we had was tiny. The flood, however, called for a bathtub-sized receptacle. Jim hauled away chunks of soaked drywall as the water intensity began to wane. I put a bunch of beach towels on the floor and we surveyed the situation. Drip. Drip. Drip.

"What do you think caused this?" I could see the distress in his eyes.

"I'm guessing it's the air conditioning unit. The drip pan is just above us in the attic. Call Right Time and ServPro. You have their numbers, don't you?"

"I do."

Right Time Home Services had recently installed a new A/C unit in our attic. Apparently... they screwed up.

"Why ServPro?" I asked.

"They need to inspect how much water damage we have, then dry it out before we get mold."

"Will insurance pay for all of this?"

"Yeah, they'll pay."

I called Right Time and ServPro. "No one can come out today. It's too late so they're sending someone tomorrow morning."

"I had a feeling that would be the case. What a racket."

I was overwhelmed. My house was a soggy mess and I had only been in it for five minutes. I wanted to twitch my nose and make it magically disappear. No such luck.

"Don't worry, Tracey." He rubbed my back. "This is not a big deal. It's fixable. No one was hurt."

"But Thanksgiving is coming soon. Let's fix this mess and take a vacation to Hawaii."

"We're not going to Hawaii. We just got home."

"I know, but ugh! I don't want to live in this mess."

"They'll clean it up before Thanksgiving and everything will be fine."

"No, they won't. And to top it off, Right Time will deny responsibility."

"I'll take care of you. I always do." Jim's words are always so reassuring, but I'm a skeptic.

The next day, a technician from Right Time, assessed the problem, then admitted to improperly installing a blower and overflow pan. *They admitted it!*

ServPro brought in drying equipment that buzzed and whined for days in the damaged area. Jim called in an adjuster. As for me, I wanted out. So for fun, I googled, 'Last Minute Vacation Spots.' The first photo that popped up lured me in.

"Check this out," I said, holding up my iPad. "It's an underwater hotel in the Maldives. We'd feel right at home. Yelp gave it four stars."

He looked at the picture. "Whoa, that's insane. You'd think a place like that would get five stars."

"They probably would—if guests were guaranteed that the dining room ceiling wouldn't cave in."

"Very funny, Tracey. We're not going."

Gifts

To kick off the holiday season, my daughter Amy sent the following text on November 15, 2018.

Dear family, with the holidays upon us and Black Friday and Cyber Monday just around the corner, I thought it helpful if you all could share anything on your holiday wish list so we can have some guided help in gift-giving this year. If there is something you've had your eye on let me know. Thank you and love you all!

Stephanie replied: Great Idea! I'll have a think and share here.

Sidebar - I love knowing what my kids want for Christmas; it makes my job easier.

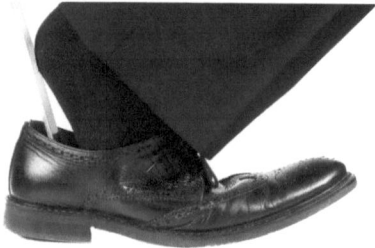

Jim replied: I'd like a long-handled shoe-horn. Getting old and need help with shoes.

My son-in-law Jason, teased Jim with a Sock Slider video, a contraption designed for challenged geriatrics. A slew of gift ideas followed: a projector for movie nights; a screen; speakers; and a popcorn maker. Grasp the theme? The final text in the chain came from Stephanie's husband, Lewis. He wrote: Scratch that, we'll regroup and get back to ya.

For whatever reason, I didn't take his text seriously and instead logged onto Best Buy and Bed Bath & Beyond. I was in full buy mode, baby!

I bought the kids projectors, speakers, popcorn makers, and, as a gag gift, a couple of Sock Sliders. I didn't consult Jim, I just did it. When I awoke Monday morning, Jim turned toward me in bed and said, "Why don't you buy the kids their gifts today, Tracey? it's Cyber Monday and you'll get huge discounts."

"I already bought their gifts," I said proudly.

"What did you buy them?"

"Everything they asked for."

"What?" Jim sat up.

"You heard me," I said.

"You literally bought them everything they mentioned in that chain of texts? The one where I asked for a long-handled shoehorn?"

"Yes," I grinned. Jim glared at me.

"Don't worry, Honey. I'll buy you a shoehorn at the 99-Cent store."

"Why the 99-Cent store, Tray?" he said with a pitiful grin.

"Because, Babe, I spent way too much on the kids."

Pets

While tutoring one day, I engaged in an interesting conversation with a fifth grader. For the sake of this story, I will call her Rain because she was unique as the day's weather.

"Rain," I said, while reading her a story about South African children who keep tarantulas as pets, "do you have a pet?"

"I had a lizard," she answered, "but when I went away to soccer camp she died."

"I'm so sorry to hear that. Have you replaced your lizard?"

"No."

"Why not?" I asked.

"Crickets."

"Crickets?" I furrowed my brow.

"Mom doesn't like noisy pets," she said. "Maybe I should get a tarantula. She might like that better."

"Wait a minute. Was your lizard noisy?"

"No, but the crickets she ate were."

I scanned the remainder of the story to see if there was any mention of what tarantulas eat. There wasn't. "Let's pause here a second, Rain, and do a quick Google search to find out what tarantulas eat, okay?"

"Okay," she agreed. Our search uncovered that crickets were the most common food of these spiders.

"No tarantula for me," said Rain, disappointed.

"If you could have any pet in the world, what would you want?"

"Hmm. Let me think. It's gotta be something mom would like, too." Rain went back to reading aloud.

"I know!" she said, raising her head from the pages of the book.

"What?" I stared into her youthful brown eyes.

"An anteater."

"Why an anteater?" I asked.

"Because ants ate mom's breakfast this morning."

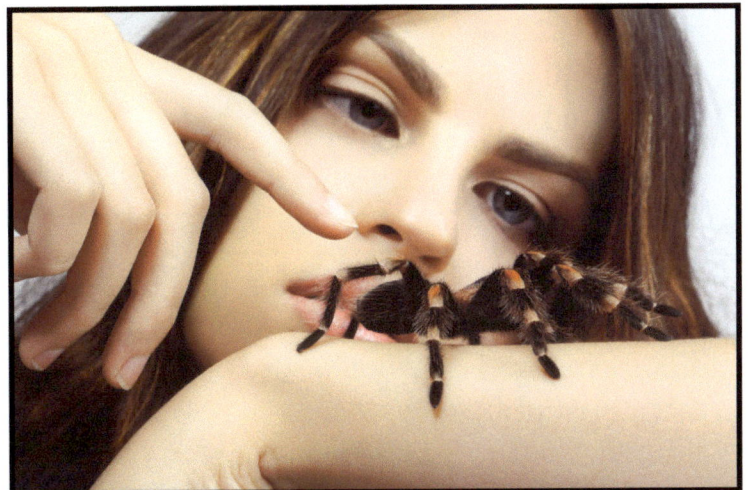

Chikele

We were headed to Cabo San Lucas, Mexico, my favorite place to buy chicklets chewing gum. I call them chikele. To prepare for the trip, I asked Jim to gather up his peso ball-markers to use as currency for the gum.

"They're worthless, Tracey," he said, "I'm not going to bring them."

"But Jim, do you know how much chikele I can buy with a handful of pesos?"

"No, amuse me. How much gum can you buy with a handful of pesos?"

"Probably six packets."

"No, I'm keeping my ball-markers."

"You don't understand," I said, defeated. Then I let the conversation go.

Upon arrival at the San Jose del Cabo Airport, we were ushered through Customs then on to baggage claim. While my eyes were glued to the revolving baggage carousel, I noticed four shiny gold and silver coins on the ground. I immediately plucked them up and slipped them

into my pocket. Now I have chikele money, I thought.

On the shuttle to our hotel, I held out my hand to show Jim the pesos. "Look what I found at the airport."

"Whoa, that's a lot of money! Buy yourself some gum when we go to dinner tonight."

Once we arrived at the Pueblo Bonito Rose, we unpacked, changed clothes, bought a beer at the corner Mercado, then sipped our way to Locos Tacos where we bought four tacos

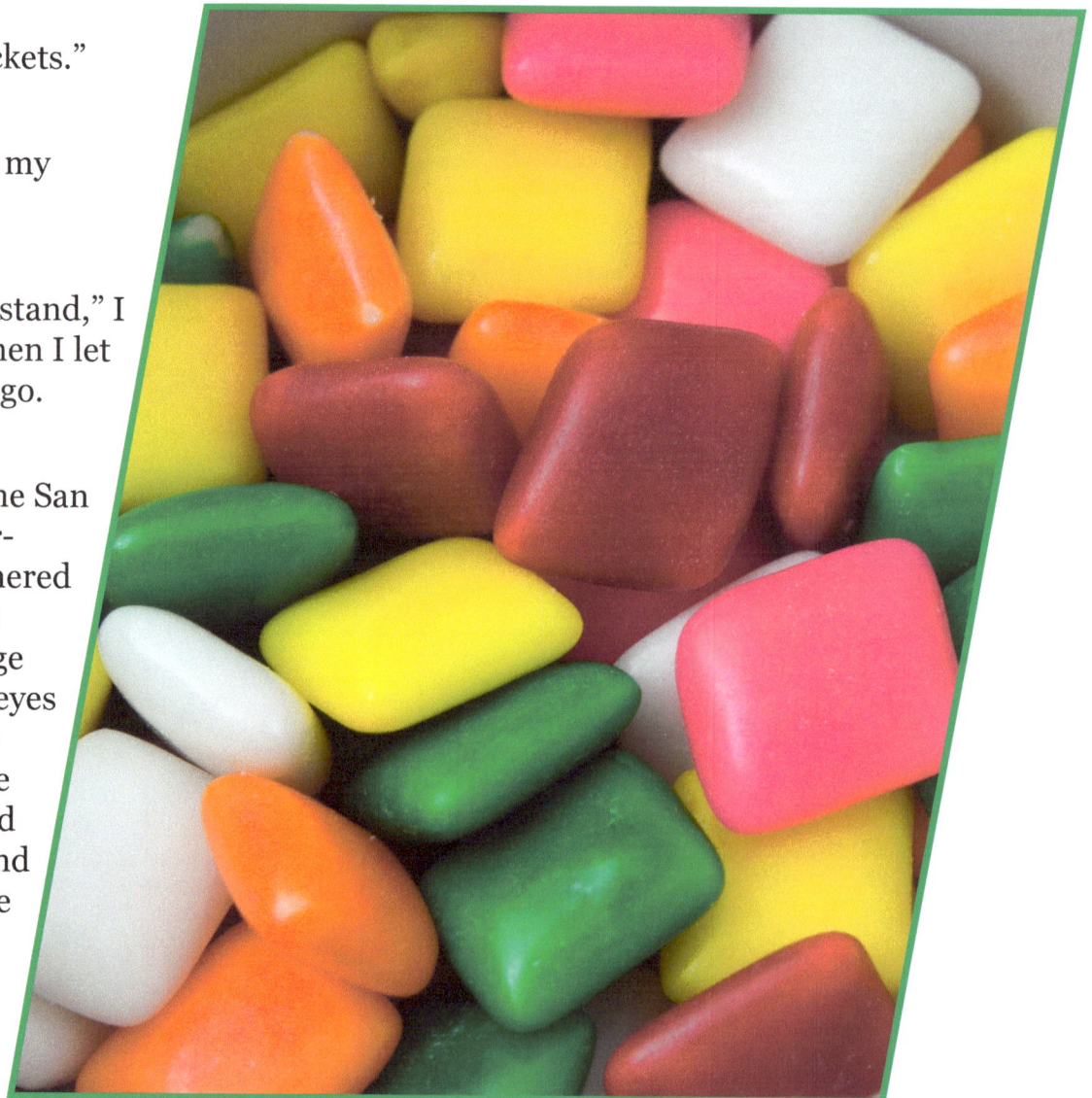

and a beer for $8. Venders were notably missing in the restaurant courtyard. "Where are all the kids selling chikele?" I said to Jim.

"I don't know, Tracey, it's been four years since we've been here. I don't see those annoying mice-on-a-string either."

After dinner as we strolled along the marina admiring the fishing boats, we came upon two small boys holding boxes of colorful chikele. "Cuanto cuesta uno (how much for one)?" I asked the boys.

"Veinte (20) pesos," answered the boy to my left. I dug into my pocket to retrieve my found loot. My pocket was empty.

"Shoot, Jim. I must have left the pesos at the hotel."

"Oh, well. Next time."

I looked at the boys' adorable faces. Their mom was sitting nearby behind a blanket of small figurines. I handed each boy a crisp twenty-dollar bill.

"Para ti," (for you) I said, smiling. Both boys offered me their entire boxes of chikele. "No gracias," I said. "Felice Navidad."

"Muchas gracias," said the boys' mom.

Six more days in Cabo and I never saw another kid selling chikele. On the plane ride home, I pulled out the coins and presented them to Jim. "For you," I said with a grin, "four shiny new ball-markers for Christmas."

HOW MUCH CHIKELE CAN YOU BUY WITH A HANDFUL OF PESOS?

Louie

Occasionally, I offer to walk my neighbor's dog. His name is Louie. On this particular night, Ann and Mark were hosting us for dinner and Canasta. After dinner, I offered to wash the dishes or take Louie for a walk on the golf course.

The fairway is a pooping palace for Louie. "Are you sure you want to take him, Tracey?" asked Ann. "You'll have to pick up his poop."

"Of course," I said, "no problem. I love Louie. I don't mind at all."

"Okay, then. Take him. He'll love it!"

Louie spun in circles when Ann picked up his leash. I clipped the leash to Louie's collar, grabbed my cell phone, and made my way outside. It was a beautiful moonlit night.

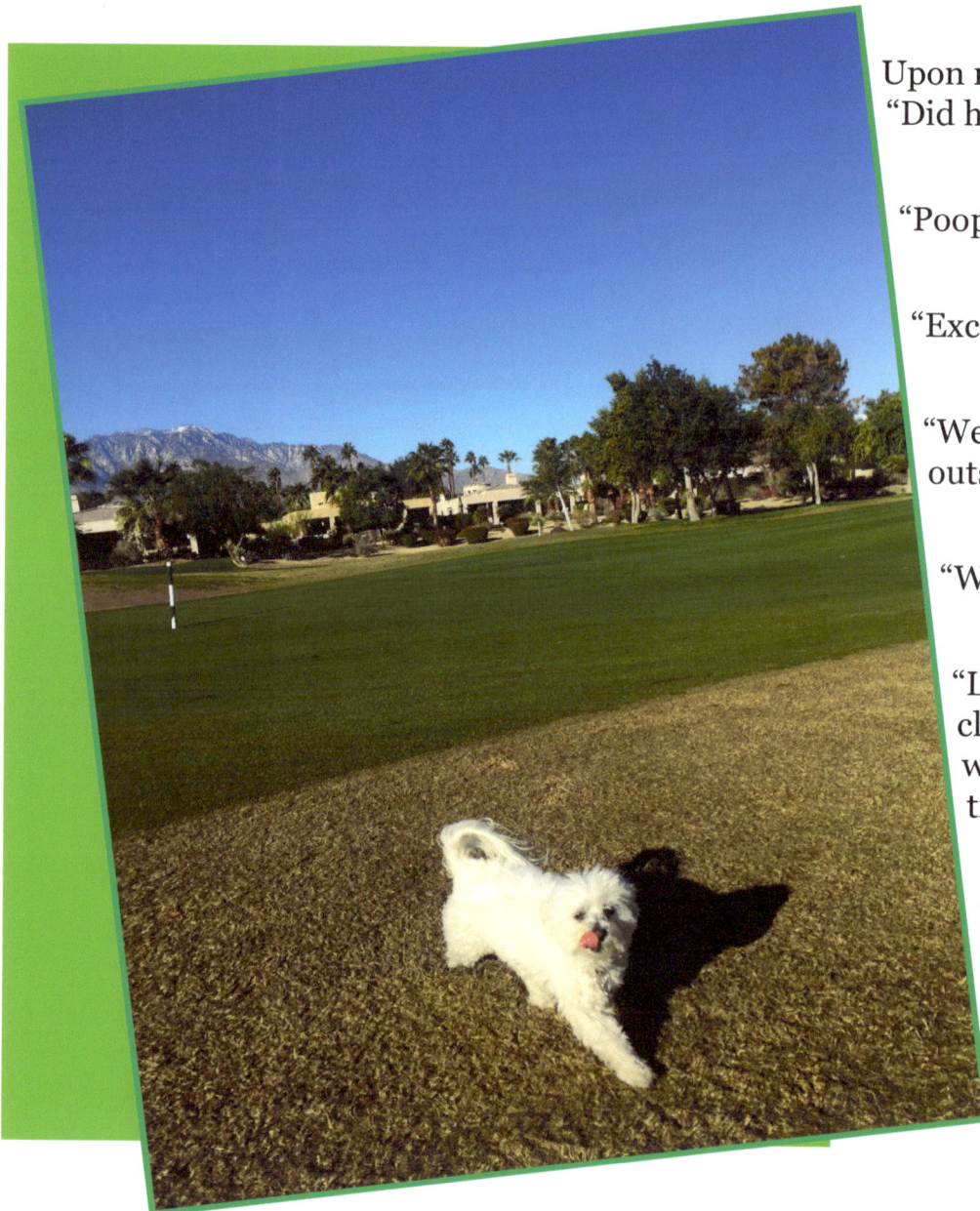

Upon my return, Ann asked, "Did he go?"

"Poop? Yes," I said, "except…"

"Except what?" asked Ann.

"We were fine until we got outside of your gate."

"What happened?"

"Louie started to run circles around me like he was wrapping a maypole. He tied up my ankles."

"He does that when he gets excited. But he stops."

"Oh really? Because he never did."

"Did you tell him to stop?"

"Of course I did. I shouted, 'Louie, STOP! I'm getting dizzy.'"

"Did you tug on the leash?"

"I did, but I became flustered and dropped my phone."

"Did it break?" she asked.

"The leash or my phone?"

"Your phone," Ann smirked.

"It landed in tall grass, so no, it didn't break. But, as I went searching for it, I noticed Louie squatting on the fairway."

"Was he pooping?" Ann was unusually focused on the completion of Louie's poop event.

"Yes, but I tugged him off his throne, so-to-speak."

"In the middle of pooping?"

"Yes. I felt horrible, but I couldn't let him poop before I found my phone. I needed my flashlight to find it and scoop it up."

"What happened after that?"

"I found my phone."

"And?"

"I turned on the flashlight and looked for Louie's poop."

"Then what?"

"I had to go home to clean Louie's shit off my shoes."

"Good dog, Louie. " Ann praised her poopy puppy.

"Next time," I snickered, "I'll wash the dishes."

"Yes, I felt horrible, but I couldn't let him poop before I found my phone."

59

Tree Talk

One of my many quirks is that I talk to plants. You already know that I talk to birds and animals, too. Doesn't everyone? Tracey in Wonderland, that's me. I play music for them, too. Songs in the tree of life, baby! One day while writing at my desk, I gazed out of my window and said, "Hiya, Palm Tree. I'm a big fan (pun intended) of yours." A slight breeze fluttered the fronds of the tree and I took that to mean 'Hello, Tray.'

A moment later, I received a text from my daughter Amy. It read: are we going to do poetry and pink champagne on X-mas this year?

Sidebar: Poetry and pink champagne is a brainchild of mine intended to inspire my family to embrace poetry. Every Christmas, we sit together on the couch and read our poems out loud. Pink champagne calms the nerves. Not everyone is as comfortable reading aloud as I am.

I replied to Amy with a Yes, Honey. It's a tradition.

I was having a little writer's block at the time, and couldn't think of anything else to say to my plants, so I decided to go in search of a poem. I flipped through a couple of my children's poetry books then found this doozy written by Jack Prelutsky.

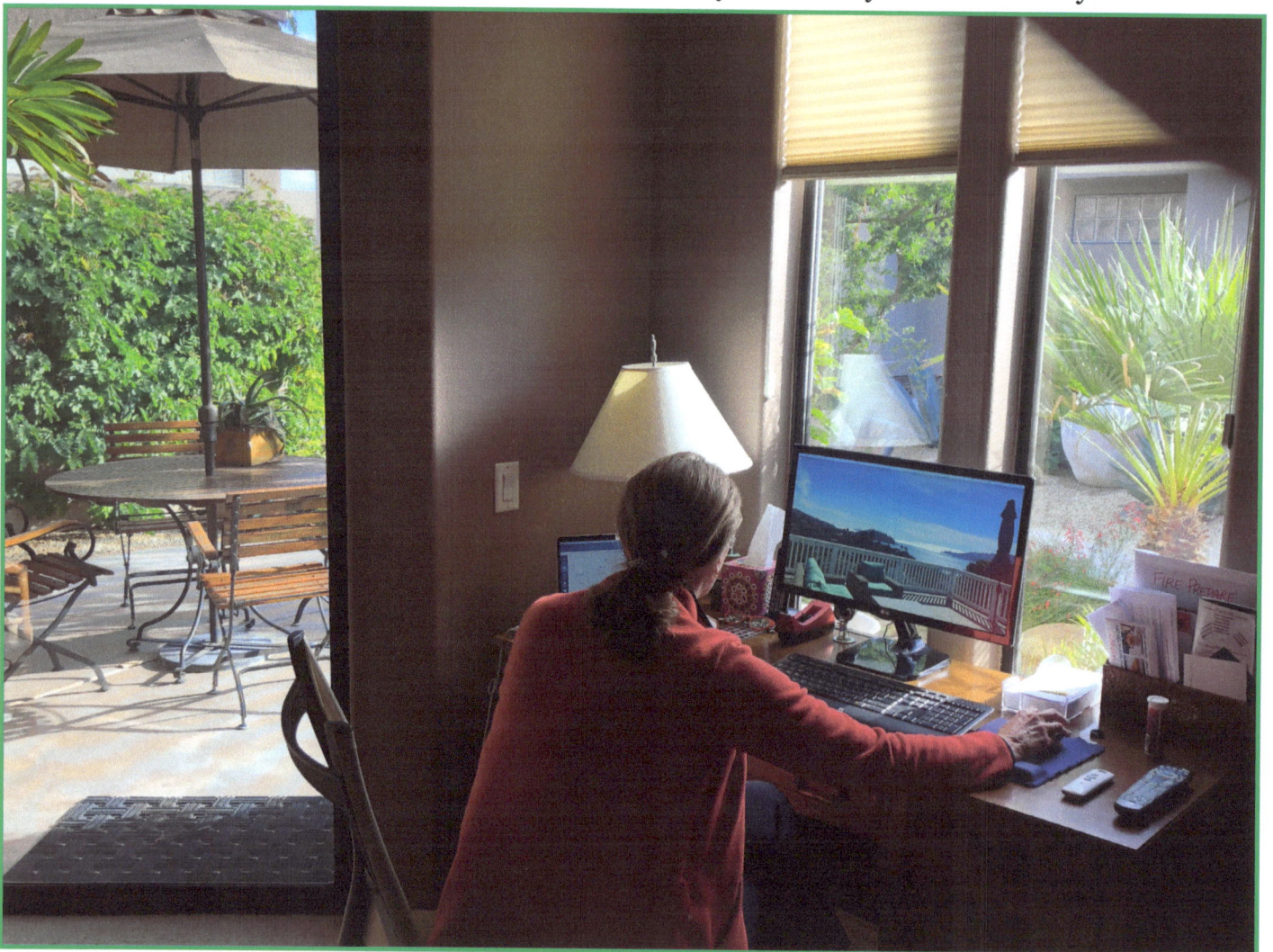

Floradora Doe
by Jack Prelutsky

Consider the calamity of
Floradora Doe,

who talked to all her plants because
she thought it helped them grow,

she recited to her ivy,
to her fennel, ferns, and phlox,

she chatted with her cacti
in their little window box.

She murmured to her mosses,
and she yammered to her yew,

she babbled to her basil,
to her borage and bamboo,

she lectured to her laurels,
to her lilac and her lime,

she whispered to her willows,
and she tittered to her thyme.

She gossiped with a poppy,
and she prattled to a rose,

she regaled her rhododendrons
with a constant stream of prose,

then suddenly, one morning,
every plant keeled over, dead.

"Alas!" moaned Floradora.
"Was it something that I said?"

Sleep Number

Jim and I sleep on a plush-performance, pressure-relieving king mattress that adjusts to our comfort on both sides by allowing us to set a 'sleep number' of our preference. My sleep number is 65. Jim prefers his side firmer at 85. Additionally, the mattress can re-shape itself into a multitude of positions. We loaded the Sleep Number app on our phones, and we were raring to go.

Last night I went to bed early to read Becoming by Michelle Obama, a Christmas gift to myself. With my Sleep Number remote, I adjusted the bed to the zero-gravity setting. Simply stated, my back and legs were slightly raised to mimic floating on a cloud. In the middle of page 23, I heard a clicking sound. What was that? I thought. My butt began to sink. Suddenly I was shaped like a taco. I checked the sleep-number remote. It still read zero-gravity. "What the hell is going on here?" I sighed. I was too tired to figure things out so I readjusted the bed to the snore position and fell asleep.

The next morning when I awoke, I felt like I had slept all night in a ditch. "Jim," I said turning to face him. "I think our bed is broken."

"Why?"

"Because last night while I was reading, my body suddenly warped."

"What the hell does that mean, Tray?"

"I mean, after hearing a clicking noise from, I-don't-know-where, my body drooped into the shape of a taco."

"A taco?"

"Yes, Jim. V-shaped. I heard a strange noise then my ass sunk and my head and legs arose."

"Oh, shit!"

"Oh, shit. What?" I said sitting up.

"It was me. I did it. I forgot."

"You did it?" I said. "How?"

"Last night while I was watching Madam Secretary, I was messing around with my Sleep Number app."

"Why did you deflate me?" I whined. "That was mean."

"That wasn't my intention," he confessed. "One of those Sleep Number commercials came on and I thought I'd lower my side while I was thinking of it. My back has been sore lately."

"Before you even got into bed?"

"Yeah," he said, "but I chose the right side of the bed."

"NO, Jim!" I argued. "You chose the wrong side. Everything of mine is on the right, remember? I'm always *right*. Everything of yours is on the *left*. Don't forget that."

We both got out of bed and rubbed our lower backs.

"Don't ever deflate me again," I said with a crooked smile. "Deflate your-self!"

I walked around the bed and kissed Jim on the cheek.

"By the way," I said, "how is your back feeling this morning?"

"The same," he replied. "It hurts."

"Swell," I complained. "Mine hurts too."

Suddenly I was shaped like a taco.

Jars

Jars. I can't open them. Fortunately for me, I have Jim.

A few summers ago in Colorado, I prepared fresh peach jam that I stored in a dozen Mason jars. Once the lids were sealed, I couldn't open any of them.

As a child, my mom had a handy jar opener. When it worked, you could hear the vacuum seal POP!—then magically, the jar would open.

I needed one of those the other day while I was whipping up a batch of Chasen's chili. Unfortunately, the recipe called for five jars of tomatoes.

As I began to prepare the ingredients, I asked for Jim's help. "Will you open these for me?" I said, holding two of the five jars.

"Of course I will." Within minutes, all five jars were opened.

Four days later, Jim came to me with the Sunday Styles section of the New York Times. He knows it's my favorite. On page five, I saw the words, "Tiny Love Stories, Our Gratitude Jar." Here is what it said:

We're supposed to open the jar on New Year's Day, hungover in our pajamas, reading the little notes of gratitude we had written to each other throughout the year. But I haven't been able to wait. Every time I saw him pause during a happy evening to write down a memory in his delicate script, I unscrewed the jar, pulled out the Post-it (despite his halfhearted protest), and smiled as I read his words: gratitude for our health, our home, our family, our dog, our friendship and love. Why wait to remind ourselves how good life is together— Colleen Goodhue

I brought the newspaper back to Jim and told him about the little love story. "There is a story about a gratitude jar in here that you should read. It's really charming."

"I know," he smiled. "I read it. That's why I brought you the paper. By the way," he said, handing me a Mason jar, "this is for you. Read what's inside."

I opened the loosely closed jar, unraveled the small piece of paper inside, and read its contents out loud.

Tracey, I am grateful for the delicious meals that you prepare for me. I especially love it when you ask me to open jars. In a small way, I feel like I've contributed to the meal. This will be our gratitude jar. If you ever need help opening it, just ask. Love, Jim.

Dancer

I was invited to be a guest judge for an 'Open Call' talent competition at the McCallum Theater. An obvious question is, Tracey, do you have talent? In my mind, I do. John Travolta doesn't hold a candle to me. And by the way, clear the dance floor when Mustang Sally comes on because I'm taking over.

On the day of the event, I picked out a dress and danced in front of my bathroom mirrored doors. Peering intently at my image, I noticed Jim walk through the door. "What time are you leaving, Tray?" I froze in place like Jennifer Beals during her audition in Flashdance. My arms were outstretched and my legs were awkwardly askew. Slowly, I drifted my body into a normal standing position.

"Uh, what?" I said, trying to appear normal.

"Were you dancing?" Jim asked. He swiveled his hips.

"Yeah."

"You're a judge, Tracey. Not a performer."

"You weren't supposed to walk in on me like that."

"You're cute, Tray. Wanna hug?"

How could I deny such a request? Jim affectionately held me in his arms while I informed him that I would be leaving the house at 3:00. When he left the room, I asked Alexa to play "The Hustle," then boogied like I was in full competition mode. "Yeah, baby!"

I arrived at the McCallum at 3:30 sharp. By 4 p.m., a parade of ballet, jazz, hip hop, and operatic performers took center stage. Is disco dead? I wondered. Disappointed that no one performed to the music from Saturday Night Fever, I drove home blasting disco music and car-danced all the way home.

Jim greeted me at the door. "How was the competition, Tray?"

"Follow me," I said, rolling my finger, "I'll show ya." I led Jim into our bedroom then pulled off my dress and tossed it onto our bed. Then, I danced around in my bra and underwear singing,

Oh yes, it's Ladies' Night/And the feeling's right/Oh yes, it's Ladies' Night/Oh what a night

Jim keenly followed my rhythmic dance moves with a smile on his face as large as a Cheshire cat. In the midst of my final spin around the room, Jim caught me with his outstretched arms.

"You win!" he boasted. Applause. Applause.

65

Pills

Prescription meds are a pain in the ass to keep track of so I memorize them by shape, size, and color. To top it off, the EZY seven-day pill case lids pop open at the most inopportune times, making it anything but easy to put them back into their compartments. Imagine a bag of Skittles breaking open and spilling into the bottom of your purse—only worse.

My daily regimen is three pills every morning, so the remainder of my EZY pill case contains sleep, nausea, and digestive aids. Xanax gets the last compartment for easy access.

Because we were headed to San Francisco, I decided to get out my Brother-P Touch label maker and label each compartment. I offered to do the same for Jim.

"Hey, Jim. I'm making labels for my pill container. Want me to label yours too?"

"Sure. I'll get you the names."

After about ten minutes, Jim brought in his pill case and a list of names.

1-2: Blood pressure.

3: Cholesterol

4-5: Beta-blocker

6: Baby aspirin

7: None of your business.

"What kind of pill is, 'none of your business,' Jim?'"

"It's none of your business, Tray. Just like it says."

"Are you taking something you shouldn't?" I asked, or (wink, wink) that little blue pill?"

"They're my pills, Tracey. If you want to label them, fine. That's how I want mine labeled."

"I hear you," I acknowledged, "however, 'none of your business' won't fit on the lid, but Viagra will."

"Very funny, Tray."

"Okay, fine," I said, respecting his privacy. "Will you at least put your pill container in a baggie like I do when we travel? Scotch tape doesn't hold."

"I'll use tape," he said. "It's fine."

After a full day of schlepping around San Francisco, we arrived at the Fairmont hotel for a much-needed rest.

I unpacked my pill holder and removed my newly-labeled nighttime pills. What a pleasure, I thought.

"Jim, did you unpack your pills yet?" I waited to hear praise for my efforts.

"Yeah, but I had a slight problem," he pouted.

"What?" I asked.

"'None of your business' fell out," he said. "The tape didn't stick."

"I hate to say I told you so. So I won't." Don't ya love that phrase?

I took a short walk to the bathroom, then came back to bed extending Jim a clenched fist.

"What's in your hand, Tracey?"

"None of your business."

Oh, what a night!

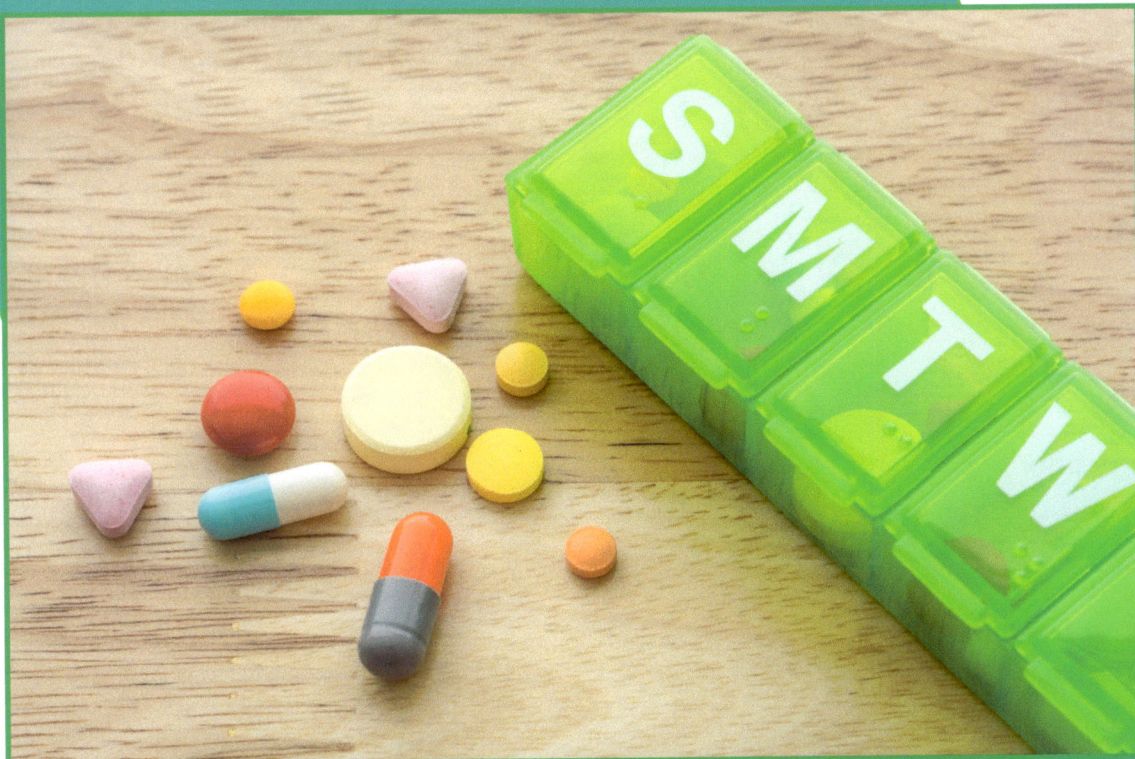

Jigsaw

Last week, I went to See's Candies in the Westfield Mall. I craved their scotch kisses and café latte lollipops. I've been sugar-addicted since childhood.

To get to See's, I had to walk through Barnes and Noble, where I stumbled upon a thousand-piece candy wrapper puzzle. It was tempting as jelly beans. "No!" I grumbled aloud, "I will not buy a candy wrapper puzzle. No. No. No!" Moments later, I made it safely to the buffet line at See's.

"I'd like a dozen scotch kisses and six café latte lollipops please," I said to the uniformed lady. She graciously handed me a chocolate sample. "Thank you," I said, taking a bite. "Yum."

I paid for my goodies then left the store. The next thing I knew, I was back at Barnes and Noble, staring at the candy wrapper puzzle.

Maybe I should buy it, I thought. Puzzles are very good for memory and brain function.

My brain could use some help, I reasoned. So, I bought the puzzle.

When I got home, I showed it to Jim.

"Look what I bought us!"

"Not us, Tray. *You*. This is all *you*."

"Won't you help me a little?"

"Nope. Knock yourself out. But I think you are nuts."

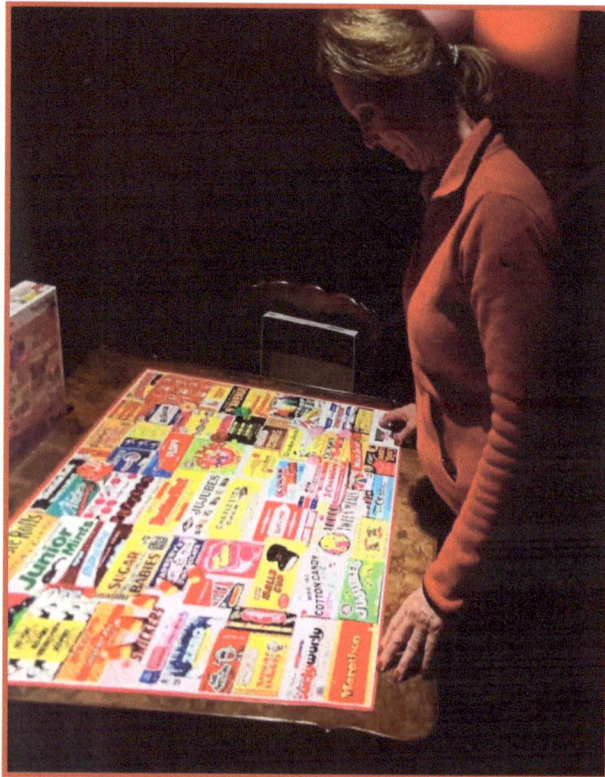

"Fine. I'll do it myself."

I sifted through the bag and pulled out all of the border pieces. I assembled the border in three hours. Then, I took out six paper plates and began to separate the pieces by the number of rounded tabs they had. One, two, three, four, none, and odd-shaped leftovers.

After two days of intermittent jigsaw separating (I have a life ya know), I went to work interlocking the puzzle pieces.

Five days later, I had all but three pieces of the puzzle in place. Those pieces were missing.

"Jim, I'm going crazy." I stood up from the game table.

"What's wrong, Tracey?"

"I'm almost done with the puzzle except I'm missing the 'nut' in coconut."

"Whaddoyamean?" he slurred.

"I mean the puzzle is finished except for the word 'nut' in the bottom right-hand corner."

"Lemme see," he said, getting up from the couch. That's when I noticed Jim put his hand into his pocket.

My detective instincts kicked in. "Did you take the nut in coconut to drive me nuts?"

"What are you talking about, Tracey?"

I pointed to the missing spot on the puzzle. "Here!" I said, "N–U–T is missing. Right here! Now show me what's in your pocket, Mister!" I demanded.

I stared into his guilty brown eyes.

"Hand 'em over," I insisted, holding out my palm.

"Nice work." He ran his hand over the puzzle and ignored my demands.

"Quit stalling," I said, placing my hands on my hips. "Give me the pieces!"

"I told you jigsaws make you nuts. He patted my back.

"No, Jim. YOU make me nuts."

"I told you jigsaws make you nuts."

He uncurled his left hand and revealed the three missing pieces. He carefully laid them into place.

"You're such a putz," I sneered.

"But I helped you do the puzzle, didn't I?"

"Ugh," I sighed, with half a smile. Then, he kissed my forehead.

Men.

DOIN OK

I recently bought a white Sport Utility Vehicle. That was a mistake. Where I live, white SUVs are as common as cataracts.

I had a panic attack in the Gelsons' parking lot, mumbling, "Is this my car? Is that my car? Shit, where is it?"

My previous car had vanity plates that read DOIN OK, but they drove away when my daughter bought the car. Jim promised me he'd get them back once Stephanie registered the car and got her own license plates. Until then, I bitched and complained. "Jim," I said, "I hate my new car."

"Why, Tray?"

"It's white."

"You chose it, I didn't."

"I know, I know, but I'm not doin' ok anymore, I'm doin' awful. When will I get my plates back?"

"When Stephanie gets her plates, you'll get yours."

"How long?" I whined.

"I don't know, but once they're here I'll take them to the DMV and put them on your new car."

"You'll go to the DMV for me?" I said, surprised.

"Yes," he assured me, "and I'll put them on your new car." Six weeks passed and finally, the plates arrived in the mail. The next day, Jim jumped into action, "I'm going to the DMV this afternoon."

"Make an appointment," I warned. "The DMV is hellish without one."

"I will," he said. "Don't worry." Jim left the house.

> Where I live, white SUVs are as common as cataracts.

Two hours later, he was back.

"You didn't make an appointment, did you?" I said. "You were gone a really long time."

"No, I didn't. But now I need a screwdriver."

"Let's have champagne!" I insisted, bouncing up and down in my chair. "I'm so happy! DOIN OK is back."

"Not a drink, Tracey," he snarled, "an *actual* screwdriver. I have to go back to the DMV so I can remove the old plates." He hastily rummaged through drawers.

"You're kidding," I was dumbfounded. "That's ridiculous."

"Don't worry," said Jim, rushing to get to the DMV before they closed. "The lady said I could cut the line if I came right back with a screwdriver."

Jim finished the task, then texted: Mission Accomplished.

My response: 💋💋

When he finally arrived home, I poured us two screwdrivers (because I have a sense of humor) with a juicy slice of orange balancing on the rim.

"DOIN OK," I said, offering a toast.

"DOIN OK 2," said Jim, tapping my glass.

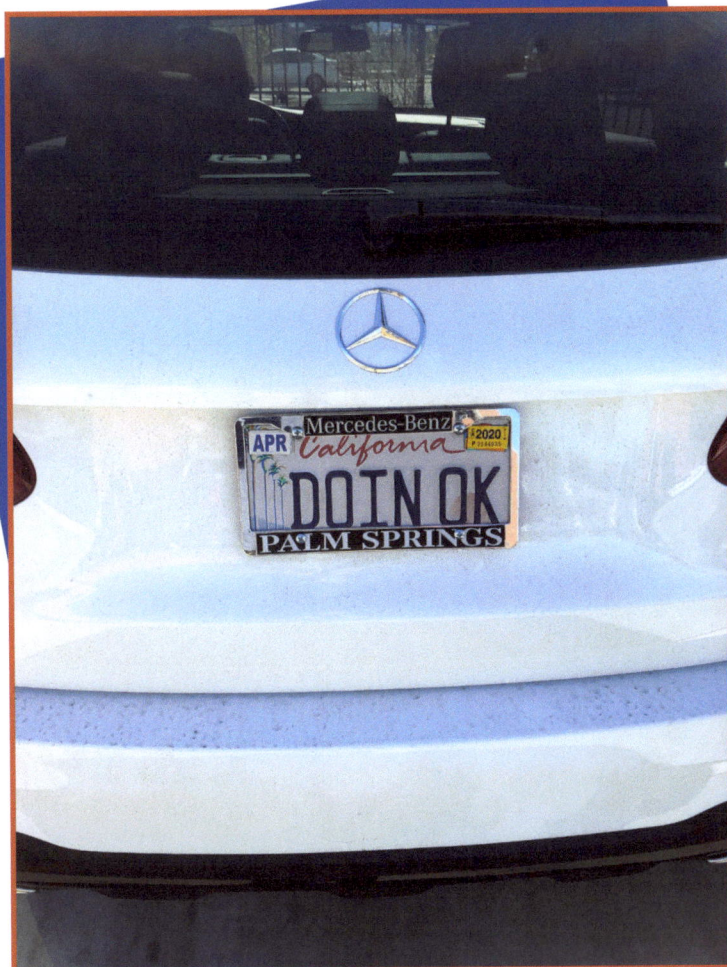

Luxurious Bath

It was a rain-soaked Valentine's Day and Jim had a golf match scheduled at PGA West. The dry riverbed in our courtyard had standing water in it. Peering wearily out of our bedroom window, I said, "I don't think you'll be playing golf today."

Jim pulled his phone off of the charger and checked his email. "You're right, Tray," he pouted. "Golf is canceled."

"I'm sorry, Honey," I said. "Would you like to go to the air museum later this afternoon?"

"No, I've got to run errands."

"Did you forget to buy me something for Valentine's Day?" I teased.

"Maybe."

"Don't fret, Cupid," I consoled him. "I only want one thing from you today."

"What do you want?"

"I want a warm bath when I get home from tutoring today."

"A bath?"

"Yes," I said, "and I'll leave it up to your imagination to make it luxurious."

"Okay, if that's what you want, I'll do it."

"Thanks, Babe. See you around lunchtime."

When I returned home from school at noon, I found Jim in our bathroom with the door closed.

"Hi, Jim. I'm home."

"Don't come in here," he cautioned. "I want it to be a surprise."

"No problem. But will you hand me a robe so I can undress for the big reveal?" Jim tossed me a robe. Minutes later, he opened the bathroom door. Inside were flickering candles, soft music by Jean-Pierre Rampal, a scent of ginger from a cup of tea, a card, and a chocolate marshmallow heart from See's.

"This looks amazing," I said sincerely, "but what's in the water?" The tub was filled with twigs, dried fruit, and flowers.

"Whatever was in the purple mesh bag," he said.

"Honey, it looks like Potpourri. Did you get the mesh bag from my underwear drawer?"

"No. It was in a basket under your sink next to the Epsom Salts. I thought that was your bath stuff."

"Oh, Honey," I reassured him, "it's perfect. Thank you."

I gave Jim a kiss and slid my body beneath the colorful array of flowers.

"You're welcome," he said, turning to walk away.

"Before you go, will you do me a favor?"

"What?"

"Will you join me?"

"I'd love to," he said, slipping out of his clothes.

Happy Valentine's Day!

Rebates

Jim was brainstorming while our handyman dismantled our master bathroom toilet. "Do me a favor, Tracey. Will you google our water district's toilet rebate program?"

"Why?" I asked.

"Michael thinks we could get a $100 rebate for installing a new toilet and $10 for recycling the old one."

"Seriously? I'm not schlepping a toilet to a recycling center for 10 bucks. I'll call for large trash pick-up."

"It's not just $10, Tracey. It's $110. If we changed all four we could save $440."

"Whoa! I'm not a math whiz, but this toilet cost over $300. Multiply that by four and you'll be spending $1,200 to maybe save $440, plus installation, plus a U-Haul to take them to the recycling center."

"They'll fit in your car," said Jim.

"Not my new car, they won't!"

"Relax. If you don't want to look it up, I will."

"Ugh."

"Think about it, Tracey. The house is 20 years old. Our toilets are beginning to sound like a chorus of 'Constipation Blues' every time they're flushed."

Jim broke my angry spell. "Is 'Constipation Blues' the name of a real song?"

"Yeah. You can google that, too, while you're at it."

"I'm not schlepping a toilet to a recycling center for ten bucks."

I did a search. The Coachella Valley Water District did offer a high-efficiency rebate and, 'Constipation Blues' is a song by Screamin' Jay Hawkins. I listened to the song. It's a hoot.

"Ok, guys," I said to Jim and Michael, "it's true. The rebates are in effect, so put the old crapper into the garage and we'll figure out a way to recycle it."

"We might as well do all four, Tray, and take one trip to the recycling center."

"Not *we* Jim. *You*."

"Fine. I'll take your car."

Michael chimed in. "I'll take them in my truck," he offered. "Not a problem."

"That's a nice offer, Michael," I said. "Thank you, but we pay you $50 an hour so…"

Jim interrupted. "Stop, Tracey. I will take them. Thanks anyway, Michael."

"We will figure this out," I assured the guys.

With one toilet installed, we awaited the arrival and installation of the remaining three.

Six days later we had all new toilets, but due to Jim's busy schedule (golf, golf, golf), our garage looked like a warehouse for old toilets. So, I decided to do something about it.

Introducing… Flower Pots by Fuller

No shit. I'm taking orders.

$110 each.

Soft Landing

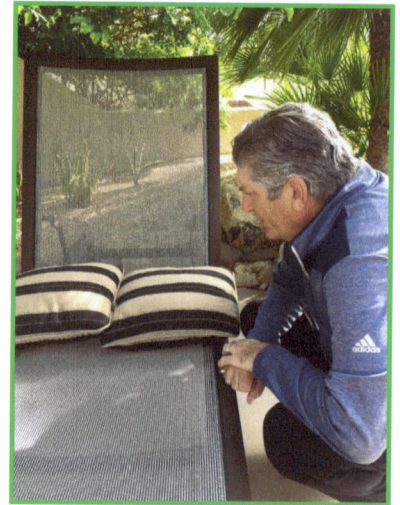

Last Sunday, a violent wind blew through our backyard. Umbrellas toppled and branches were ripped from trees. Once the storm had passed, Jim grabbed a rake and some pruning shears then headed outside.

"Babe," I said, "keep an eye out for nests. We have a few nesting birds."

"I'm just going to remove small branches that hang over our dining table because birds keep shitting on it," he said.

"I know, but birds are nesting around there, so look carefully. That's all I ask."

"I will, I will," he said, dismissively. Suddenly, he yelled, "Tray, come here!" I ran to the yard.

"There's a hummingbird nest right here." He pointed to a low-hanging branch on our Minneola tree. I grabbed my camera.

"Don't scare her," I warned. "She's probably been traumatized by the haboob."

"Haboob-schmoob," he scoffed. "She's a bird, Tray. She can fly."

"But her eggs can't fly. They'll just fall on the ground and go splat!"

"They're fine."

"That wind was brutal, Jim. I'll talk to her and calm her down."

"Go ahead. Talk to her. But she doesn't need you—she's a bird."

"Just because you don't talk to birds doesn't mean ..."

"I don't need to," Jim justifed.

We left for Carlsbad, uncertain about the fate of our hummingbirds. When we came home, I made a beeline for our backyard to check on the nest. That is when I saw the most miraculous sight—a baby hummingbird had fallen from its nest and landed on pillows. It was alive.

"Jim," I yelled, someone moved our lounge chair directly beneath the nest and a baby fell onto the pillows. She's alive. Come see. It's a miracle!"

"So my plan worked," he said, walking out to the yard.

"You? *You* put the lounge chair and pillows beneath the nest before we left for Carlsbad?"

"Yes."

"Oh, my God," I sighed. "I love you."

Jim leaned in close to the fledgling and said, "You're gonna be okay, little bird."

Look who's talking to birds now.

Buzz Off

"Tracey," said Jim, looking up from a book titled *A Thousand Places to See before you Die.* "Let's go to Vietnam."

"But Jim," I complained. "I don't like long flights, crowds, or bugs."

"Before you decide, listen to this description: *It is said that dragons once descended from heaven and spouted streams of jade droplets that fell into the waters of Halong Bay, forming thousands of islands and islets to protect the bay and its people from invading marauders.*"

My takeaway from this snippet was that mosquitos would descend from the heavens, land on my body, and spout streams of my blood into Halong Bay. "Honey, let's go somewhere else. Vietnam doesn't want us. They describe us as invading marauders."

"What are you talking about?"

"Marauders," I repeated. "That means bandits, looters, prowlers."

"I *want* to go there." He closed the book.

"What about the bugs?"

"What are you worried about, Tracey?"

"Mosquitos, ticks, and biting flies. Remember Africa? They ate me alive."

"This time," he advised, "spray your clothes ahead of time. Don't worry."

"But insect repellent is toxic and it makes me gag. Cough! Cough!

"Stop, Tracey!" So, I did what I usually do when I get frustrated. I googled, "How to keep mosquitos from biting you in Vietnam."

Advice #1: *Wear insect repellent.* I thought, Duh!

Advice #5: *Befriend a gecko lizard!'* I thought... interesting.

Advice #6: *Use mosquito netting.* I thought— yes!

"Hey, Jim, I figured it out! I'll take a lizard with us to Vietnam, and wear a net over my face."

"A lizard? he snorted. "Are you crazy?"

"Okay, fine. I won't bring a lizard, but I'll definitely wear the net over my face. People will think I'm a bee-keeper."

"Buzz off," he said, swatting the air. "We'll discuss this later."

I drove straight to Dick's Sporting Goods.

Check out my new purchase.

Bull Bonding

A mangy bull was shading himself beneath a row of conifer trees. His owner, a toothless man wearing tattered sandals held a rope that was tethered to the bull's nose.

Once I overcame my fear to mount the big bull, I leapt right up. "Ready!" I said, spreading my arms and legs in a spirited wave. His wooly hair was prickly, and his back was bony and parched.

I patted his hump and begged, "Please don't buck me off."

His handler shouted "di nao, di nao," which meant 'let's go' in Vietnamese. We hobbled along. His hooves were either rustling through dry leaves or squishing manure.

"Dung, dung," I alerted the bull as he sauntered along the trail. I was hoping the animal would stop stepping in his shit. No luck.

"Di nao," repeated his handler. The bull barely moved.

I kicked him like a horse, hoping he would pick up the pace. As he began to move with a little more gusto, I kept warning him, "Dung! dung!" Do you know how Bull responded?

Squish, squish.

"The way you say 'dung' Miss Tracey—bull won't go," said his owner.

"Why?" I asked the toothless man.

"He thinks you mean stop," he said. "Bull listen. Won't move." I had to laugh. Must have been my accent.

My final expression of solidarity was to pat the bull on his head and place my hat between his horns. "We get each other, don't we, Bull?" His head bobbed up and down as though he was answering me favorably. Either that or he wanted to lose the nose ring.

I dismounted my animal friend and watched him walk back to the shade of the conifer tree like a sloth. As he turned to glance back at me, I noted a twinkle in his eye.

No bull, we bonded on that ride. I'm sure of it.

I miss the bull, but not the bullshit.

Kissing

In a Buddhist monastery in Hue, Vietnam, I asked my friend Debbie if she would take a picture of me and Jim.

"We're going to kiss, okay? It's a tradition." The two of us sat down in front of a brightly lit altar and awaited Debbie's call to action.

"When!" said Debbie. We began a long lingering kiss. "Got it. But there might be a slight haze over your faces from trails of burning incense."

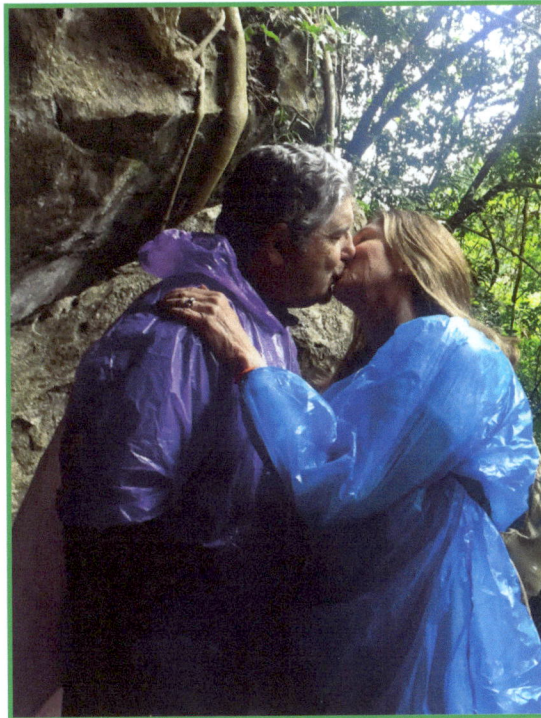

"Thanks, Deb." I reviewed the shot. "It's a little blurred, but we'll take more."

On a speed boat excursion in the South China Sea, I asked Debbie to take another kissing picture of us. "One more Deb." I handed her my phone.

"Sure."

"Say when." I prepared for the shot. We huddled together at the stern of the boat while sprays of salty water fell gently upon our heads.

"When!" said Debbie. We began our kiss. "Got it. But it may be a little blurry from sprays of water."

"That's okay, Debbie. We can take more."

On a long muddy hike along Halong Bay, we climbed through a rocky rainforest beneath a canopy of swollen banana tree leaves. When we arrived at Trinh Nu Cave, I asked Debbie to take another kissing picture of us.

Suddenly, in the middle of our photoshoot, Debbie screamed, "Bat!"

However, I misunderstood her warning and instead commented, "I'm not wearing a hat."

"I didn't say hat," she clarified, "I said bat."

"Where?" I looked around the cave.

"Over your heads," she announced.

"We'll consider him mistletoe." I pulled Jim in for a kiss.

"I got a good one," said Debbie.

"Are you sure it's not bat-blurry?"

"I'm sure," she reassured me.

Finally.

79

Climb

As we drove through the city center, our guide Ra (pronounced Raw) turned toward us to explain the day's activities.

"Fulla Group," he said, "our trip today is to waterfall. Mountain Man meet us at base of thousand steps. He take us up. He tell us about native area and make sure tree branch and rock not in path."

Sacred Peak of Phnom Kulen Mountain, Siam Reap, Cambodia.

"A thousand steps?" I complained. "We need to climb a thousand steps to see a waterfall? Really?"

"Yes, Miss Fulla," said Ra, reassuring me. "It no problem fa you."

"Isn't there a chair lift?" I asked, joking.

"No," said Ra. "No worry. Mountain Man know route. He make safe for us."

"Are there wild animals in the park?"

"No, no, no," he said, "only butterfly, bird, bull, maybe bat in tree. They no bother. Tree bark make good medicine. Mountain Man show you."

Do all things in this Vietnamese jungle begin with a "B?" I wondered.

"Can we take some medicine home?"

"What you mean?" asked Ra.

"Medicine. I might need some after climbing a thousand steps."

"You no need, Miss Fulla," said Ra. "You be fine."

The Van swerved and lunged and bumped its way to the base of the mountain. I stepped out of the van and looked to my left.

"Are we walking up those?" I said, pointing to a tower of steps flanked by two gigantic elephant sculptures.

"Yes," Miss Fulla," said Ra, "those them. Temple on top. You can pray to Buddha when you get there."

"Could you send Buddha down here please? I need to pray now."

"Not a problem fa you, Miss Fulla," said Ra. "You in good shape."

We began to ascend the steps. The higher we went the steeper they got.

"Stop!" I whined, after thirty or so steps. "I need to catch my breath."

My friend John descended a few steps to give me some sage advice. "Breathe in through your nose and out through your mouth."

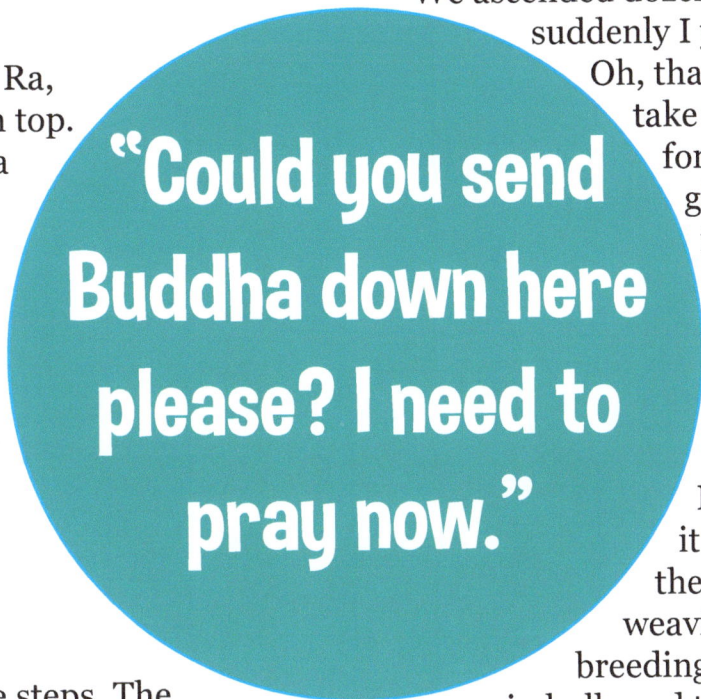

"Could you send Buddha down here please? I need to pray now."

Deep inhale. Long exhale. "C'mon Tray," said Jim, egging me on.

"Just admiring the view," I panted.

"I'm so glad I'm working out with Mark," bragged Jim. "He really prepared me for a hike like this."

We ascended dozens of more steps when suddenly I yelled, "I see Buddha! Oh, thank God." I paused to take in the majesty of its form and size. "Honey, give Buddha an offering."

"Buddha," he said. "Take my wife."

Eventually, we all made it to the waterfall. Along the way, we saw villagers weaving baskets, breeders breeding butterfly, bats hanging in hollowed tree bark, colorful birds, a bull, and a bottle of beer.

Do you know what I got out of all of this?

Another "B" word.

Blisters.

PhoNatic

I consider myself a word fanatic. Pronunciations, spelling, and grammar are important to me.

While traveling around Vietnam, I became a very good listener and observer, always trying to grasp the essence of what I was hearing and seeing.

On a tour of the Mekong region, we had a guide named Kim. She spoke in broken English, but I understood her quite well.

"Kim," I said, "What does phuc mean? Because I see Phat Phuc on signs all over the place with Buddha floating in a cloud, and I would think that's kind of insulting to Buddha."

"I tell you," she said. "If name of boy, it mean blessing."

"But these look like restaurant signs, not Amber Alerts in search of a boy named Phat Phuc."

Laughter broke out in the van.

I continued my inquisition as I steadfastly noted every phunny word I laid eyes on.

"What about, Phuc Long? Is that a name too?"

"I tell you," she said. "That mean highly blessed."

"I can agree with that interpretation."

More laughter.

"Are we on restaurant row?"

"What you mean?" she said.

"Well, I see a sign that reads Ca Phe Wifi, and I think it's intended to be English, but it's written in Vietnamese."

"I not sure what you mean, Tracey. Could you repeat that?"

"Sure," I said, pointing to a rustic sign in front of a shack. "That sign says Pho Bo Bi Que, so I assume that is a Pho barbeque restaurant, right?"

"Yes," said Kim, acknowledging my cleverness. "Bo mean beef, Bi mean go, and Que mean Thai basil. Vietnamese people eat Pho all day. Make at home, too."

"Okay," I said, gaining an understanding of the lingo.

The van swerved through hordes of Vespa's, bikes, pedestrians, and Cyclos. I was getting

"I see Phat Phuc on signs all over the place."

82

nauseous turning my head to capture all of the phunny signs.

Alongside a vendor on the highway was a sign that read, Bi Mai Phit. If she were in America, no one would stop, but in Vietnam, the locals were flocking to buy her Phit.

We continued the trek through small towns and rice fields. Along the way, I saw "Non Phat" restaurants, "Viet Cheap" dealers and other places that served "No Tran Phat" food. It was a gastronomic dream ride. All senses were firing and I couldn't wait for lunch.

"Are we almost there?" I asked as we roared down the highway.

"Yes," said Kim. "We go to Secret Garden for lunch today."

"Secret Garden? What the phuc!" (Meaning: What a blessing, I'm hungry.)

"Miss Tracey, you phunny."

Feng Shui

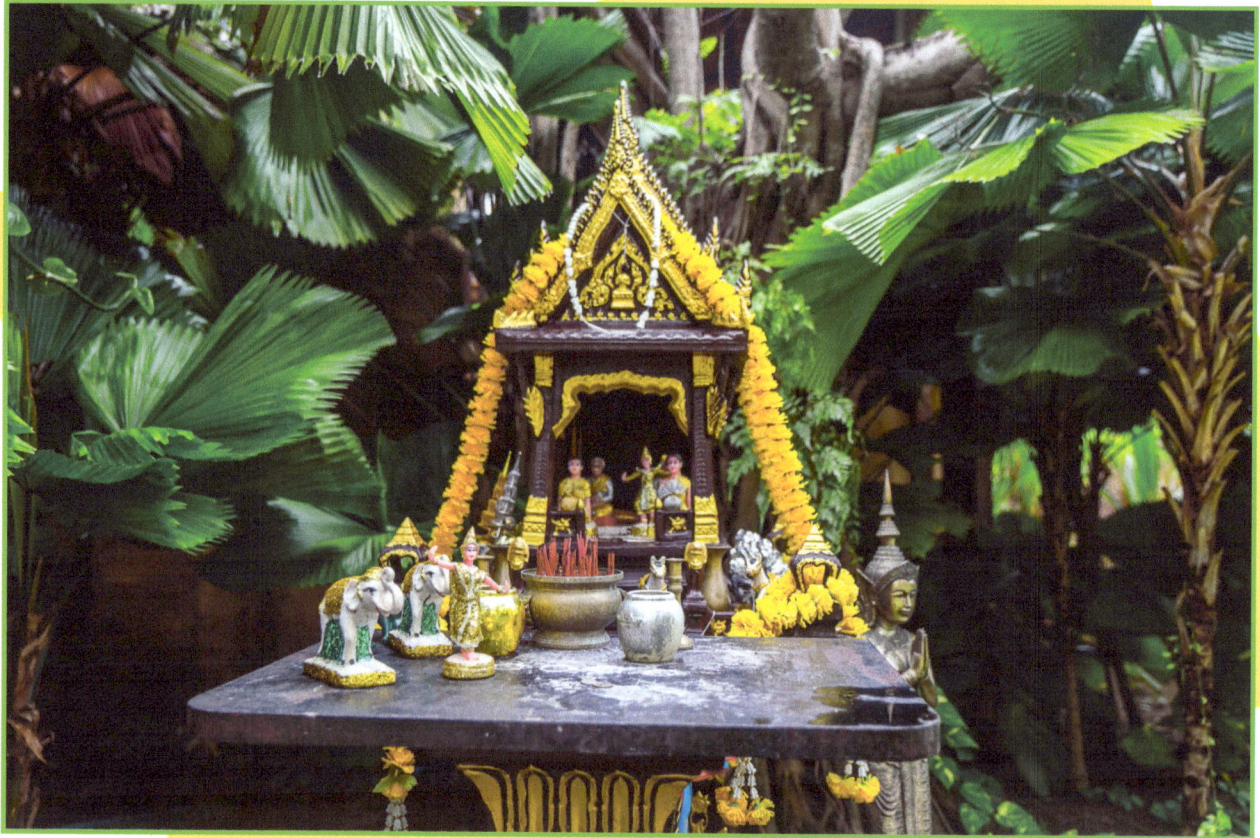

After eighteen days of traveling in Vietnam, I began thinking about constructing an ancestral shrine in my house with candles, fruit, and incense. Then, in keeping with Vietnamese traditions, I would have something to bow to when I enter my home and pay homage to my deceased loved ones.

I proposed the idea to Jim.

"Honey, let's construct an ancestral shrine by our front door like the Vietnamese do so we can reconnect with our parents."

"No," he said bluntly.

"Okay," I said begrudgingly. "Then can we put two Gargoyles on either side of our front door to scare off evil and bring luck?" Apparently, some Gargoyles divert rainwater, too."

"Stop, Tray."

This conversation was taking place while we were unpacking from our long trip. However, when Jim says, 'stop,' I go.

"Then if I can't have a shrine or statues, I want to make our home Feng Shui."

"I'm tired, Tracey," he said. "Can we discuss this later?"

It took several days to get through all of our dirty laundry. The experience was tedious and unpleasant. Some-time later, I reintro-duced the subject by saying, "Jim, according to the laws of Feng Shui, we should paint the laundry room green because the color is calming and inspiring."

"You've got to stop this, Tracey," he said dis-missively.

"I mean it. I want to liven up our laundry room. I'll pick out some sample colors to-morrow."

"No, Tray."

"Yes, Jim."

"No!"

Dunn Edwards had lovely green hues to choose from. I chose Candy Apple Green because I love candy apples. I brought home a gallon, a tarp, and a brush.

Jim looked into my Dunn Edwards bag. "You can't be serious. Don't even think you're painting this yourself."

"Can we put two Gargoyles on either side of our front door?"

"I'll call Ruperto. He'll do the job in an hour."

"You're gonna Feng Shui me to death."

"No, I won't. But I'll be a happy wife, and you know what they say about a happy wife, don't you?"

"Yeah, Tray," he said, aggravated. "Happy wife, happy life."

"You got that right."

Go Green!

Appliances

"Babe!" I screamed, attempting to drown out the dishwasher. "This kitchen is twenty years old. It's time for us to buy new appliances."

"I hear you, Tracey," he said. "You don't have to yell, but…"

"No buts," I argued, "it's time. I'm going to Fergusons tomorrow. Wanna go?"

"Sure," he said coyly.

"Great, it's almost Memorial Weekend. We can bargain hunt."

The next day, we drove the short distance to the showroom. "This fridge is sexy, isn't it Jim?" I pointed to a Sub-Zero Pro 48 with a glass door.

"Yes, it is, but you're in the most expensive section in the store," he noted. "Follow me."

I didn't. Instead, I opened ovens, microwaves, and cabinets. I admired stovetops, range tops, hoods, and even flooring. Everything was so new and pretty. I smoothed my fingers over a slab of Cambria quartz. "This is gorgeous," I mumbled. "I wonder what this costs?"

In the distance, Jim turned to see if I was following him.

"Stay focused, Tracey. We're not replacing countertops."

"Fine." I continued to admire (fantasize) about my new kitchen remodel. "Oh, my God, this stuff's expensive."

"I know. This was your idea, not mine."

"Tacos!" I said, stumbling onto a tray of the Mexican delights. "I wonder if these are for customers."

A woman approached. "Help yourself," she said kindly.

When we finished our tacos, Jim waved me over to the Kitchen Aid and GE Profile section. But once again, I was distracted by an expensive-looking cooktop. "Blue knobs!" I said, excitedly. "I want these."

Moral of the story: Take a man shopping where free food is being served and he'll be like putty in your hands.

"This is Thermador's new line," said the lady. "They're offering a great promotion. Buy a refrigerator, wall oven, and cooktop, and receive a ventilating hood and dishwasher for free."

I turned to look for Jim. He was grabbing a cookie from another kitchen display.

"Jim, let's buy Thermador."

He twirled his thumbs, meaning it's time to go. I ignored the gesture. Instead, I asked the saleslady, "Are you open on Memorial Weekend?"

"Yes, we are," she said.

"Will you be serving BBQ ribs?"

"As a matter of fact," she said, "we are." That caught Jim's attention.

"Okay, you got me, I'll come back with you on Memorial Day."

Moral of the story: Take a man shopping where free food is being served and he'll be like putty in your hands.

Lucky me.

Redecorating

Jim always has his opinions where decorating is concerned. He is, after all, the son of a New York Interior Designer. But in this house, I have veto power. Here is how Jim and I discussed our latest redecorating project.

"Tray," he said, "I gotta say something about this project."

"I'm listening."

"Your decorating choices are..." he paused for effect, "so... monochromatic. They lack pizazz."

"Pizazz? What are you talking about?"

"I want some color in the house," he emphasized. "Please don't dress the house as you dress yourself."

"Are you insulting my fashion sense?"

"No. But you do wear monotone clothes a lot."

"I know, but I always add a pop of color with shoes, scarves, and handbags."

"True," he acknowledged, "I love the way you dress. I'm sorry."

"It's okay." I forgave him. "I wish your mom were here to help."

"Me too. She could decorate with her eyes closed."

"I'm putting together a storyboard of textiles, so when I'm finished you can comment, okay?"

"Fine. But I want color."

"I want my house to feel like a spa."

First I looked at porcelain, wood, and vinyl floor tiles. A saleslady from Bedrosian Tile and Stone offered to help me with samples. "What style are you thinking of?" she asked.

"Spa," I said, "I want my house to feel like a spa at a five-star resort."

"A spa?" she said. "Light or dark?"

"Light. I want the whole house to feel light and airy. Oh yeah, and I want it to smell like lavender."

"Sounds lovely," she said with an awkward grin, "but all of our tiles are unscented." We laughed, and then she escorted me to the warehouse.

"Holy Cow! How am I supposed to choose?"

"You'll know it when you see it," she said. "It will feel like a perfect fit."

"You mean like shoes?"

"Yeah, just like shoes." She walked away.

About fifteen minutes later she returned. "I like this and this and this," I said, pointing to my favorites.

Within minutes she brought out a cart weighted down with samples.

"I'll help you put them in your car," she offered. Once the tiles were loaded, I drove them home and made a storyboard of ideas to show Jim.

"What do you think?" I said when he came home from golf.

"Where's the color?" he asked.

"Hold on." I ran to my closet.

A few seconds later I dropped shoes onto the board.

"There. Color. Got the picture?"

"Yeah, yeah," he shrugged. "I got the picture."

I Talk Derby

Last Saturday, I celebrated Derby Day at the Four Seasons Denver with my daughter Amy. She recently became the Director of Public Relations for that luxury hotel.

As we wandered onto the pool deck, Amy began shooting photos of the arriving guests. We galloped around a sea of hats, heels, and hunks. Click. Click. Click.

"Amy," I said, pointing to the bar. "Let's get Julep'd."

"Mom," she said, bug-eyed. "I'm working."

In a flash, I zigzagged to the bar and ordered a mint julep.

"Honey." I extended my drink. "Want to taste?"

"Maaaaa," she repeated, "I'm working."

"Oh, yeah. Sorry." Sip. Sip. I took a few pictures of my own.

"Mom, please don't take the same photos as I do. Our guests will think we're creepy voyeurs."

"I'm sorry, Honey. I don't mean to interfere, but have you noticed how many men are wearing lilac shirts and black jackets? Are they in the band?"

"Mom," she whispered. "They're security. Pretend you don't know. I'll be right back."

"Okay, but can we take a selfie first?"

"Sure." We posed for the shot.

"Thanks, Honey. The race is starting soon so hurry back."

"I will."

I watched as my daughter sprinted through a maze of men in wild print jackets haplessly flirting with women wearing fascinators dipped over their eyebrows. With television sets anchored above everyone's heads, I suddenly heard a familiar phrase, "And... they're off."

Party-goers raised their cocktails and grunted, "Go, Max! C'mon Tax!"

Max who? Tax what? Is this a horse race or a political rally? I wondered.

Minutes later, the race was over. Maximum Security had won the Kentucky Derby.

"Let's get Julep'd"

"Amy!" I yelled across the pool. "Did you hear? Maximum Security."

"Mom, stop!" She raisied her arm and shot me an evil eye. I was confused. Why was she mad at me for telling her who won the race? I guessed that she had missed it.

Amy made her way back to me.

"Mom, why did you yell 'maximum security' across the pool? Why would you do that?"

"Because that's the name of the winning horse."

"What is?"

"Maximum Security."

"You're not invited next year, Mom."

"You missed the race didn't you, Honey?"

"Yes. I did. I was taking a picture of the Ketel One wall."

"Now do you want a drink?" I said, half-joking.

Minutes later the TV announcer proclaimed, "Due to the disqualification of Maximum Security, the new winner of the Kentucky Derby is Country House." Amy heard that update.

"Whoa, Mom. You were right. Sorry I got mad at you."

"It's okay, Sweetheart. It was just a weird coincidence."

The crowd dispersed and Amy was off duty, so we sashayed over to the bar and ordered a couple of juleps.

"To next year's Derby Day at the Four Seasons." I tapped her glass. "And I promise Honey, no more horsing around."

Bamboo TP

The other day at Firehouse Subs I said to my husband, "Honey, bamboo products keep popping up as sponsored ads on my Instagram page."

"What do you think that means?" he asked.

"I'm not sure, but I was talking to our gardener about planting bamboo, and I think my phone was spying on me. Not to mention, after we spoke I had a sneeze attack that kick-started bamboo ads by a company called 'Who Gives a Crap.'"

"Do you really think Instagram is keeping track of your nose-blowing habits?"

"Maybe, I don't know." Just then I had an urge. "Be right back. I'm going to the washroom."

When I returned to the table I went on to Instagram. "Oh, my God, Jim, my page is now flashing ads for bamboo toilet paper, but this paper is absolutely adorable. It's called, No2. Isn't that clever? It is individually wrapped toilet paper rolls in great-looking colorful prints."

"Did you have your phone with you on the toilet?"

"Yes, I did. I scrolled through some stuff."

"Then yeah, I guess you are being tracked."

"You're joking, right?" I grabbed one of Jim's potato chips.

"No, Tray. When you take your phone into the crapper, you're up shit's creek."

"Don't tease me. I'm dead serious."

"Give me a minute. I'll read the ad." I handed Jim my phone.

"Number 2," he read aloud, "your #1 toilet paper. 100% bamboo, butt-crumble-free, silky and stylish. Welcome to an easy switch, a big impact, and a better wiping experience. GoNo2.com."

"See, Jim? It's telling me to 'go number two.' It must know."

"You're so full of shit, Tracey."

"That's my point."

"Buy some, then. It's very pretty, but keep your phone out of the bathroom from now on will ya?"

"I will." I lied. I ordered two dozen No.2 rolls of 100% bamboo toilet paper, and I felt great. When the package arrived, I told my husband, "Did you know that bamboo curbs carbon emissions?"

Do you know what he said?

"It's not going to stop your gas, Tracey, if that's what you're thinking."

"You never know. It might." Wink.Wink.

"No Tray. When you take your phone into the crapper, you're up shit's creek."

Clean Sweep

My husband and I watch the Super Bowl with divergent interests; I like the commercials, he likes the stats. And because Jim pays such close attention to the game, I become background noise. Jim grabbed a handful of Doritos. Many fell to the ground.

"Use a napkin, would ya?" I demanded.

"C'mon, Gladys," he yelled as he leaned toward the TV. "Sing slower."

"What are you talking about, Jim?"

"I need Gladys Knight to drag out the anthem so it lasts 110 seconds."

"You're timing the length of the anthem?"

"Yeah, Tray, I am."

"What the hell for?"

"Bruce and I have a bet."

"Swell." I turned my attention to our area rug. "Did you also bet on how many Doritos would fall on the carpet?" No answer. He was too busy fist-pumping.

"C'mon baby, tails! Yes! Two down, two to go."

"Two of what?"

"Bets. Bruce and I made four bets." (Bruce is our accountant)

"Hey, there's Giselle!"

"What about her?"

"Did you notice how many times Giselle was on screen?"

"Why would I?" Jim leaned in to grab another handful of Doritos. Several more dropped to the floor.

"Because, Tracey, that's one of our bets."

"Lift your feet," I said. "There are more Doritos on the floor than in the bowl." I used my napkin to pick up the chips then left the room.

On Monday morning, Jim rolled over in bed and said, "I'm sorry I was so rude to you during the Super Bowl. I got caught up in the moment."

"You behaved like a slob."

"I know and I'm sorry."

Later that afternoon Jim came home with a brand new wireless Fuller floor sweeper.

"It had my name on it," he conceded.

"Put it to good use, Mister."

Floating

A warm desert breeze lulled me to sleep in the dim light of sunset. I was floating on a raft in my pool when suddenly I heard, "Quack! Quack!"

"You two have been here before," I said, staring at the birds. "But I'm warning you, my husband will not allow you to swim in his pool. I'm much nicer." Strangely, they were unmoved by my admonition. They kept paddling around like they owned the place. Jim heard me talking to someone outside and came to see who it was. When he saw ducks in the pool, he started flailing his arms around and yelling 'get outta there.'

"You scared them. They just wanted some privacy. I think they were about to 'fowl' around," I joked.

"They can 'fowl' around in somebody else's pool because if you let them stay, they'll keep coming back."

I felt a little guilty for being so nice to these two. I've seen them before and just yapped away like I usually do when I see birds.

"I'll get us a gator guard," he said. "That'll stop them."

"Gator as in alligator?"

"Yeah, Tray. The inflatable kind."

"Oh, and what will that do, exactly?"

"It will keep them from landing in our pool."

"But they landed in the Jacuzzi."

"I'll buy two then."

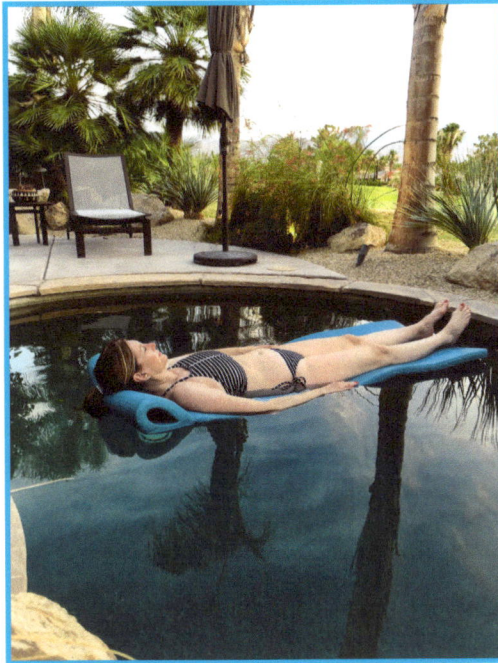

I dried off, then followed Jim into the house to see what he meant by gator guards. He showed me an image on his phone. "No way, Jim, I don't want those prehistoric creatures with blood-red eyes floating in our pool. They're terrifying."

"That's the point. The ducks will think twice before jumping in."

"No," I reminded him. "They are jumping in to keep me company."

"Ugh," he sighed.

"I'm going back into the pool." I walked out the door and gracefully slid onto the raft again. I took a slow glide around the perimeter of our pool.

Guess who was lurking behind a large boulder?

"Quack! Quack!"

Mirror

In the bedroom that I am remodeling, there is a huge mirror. The good news—it makes the room appear larger. The bad news — there is a huge mirror in my bedroom.

"Jim," I said, "I think we should get rid of the mirror."

"But," he argued, "I like the way it opens up the room. I want to keep it."

To dodge a controversy, I made a request. "Then I want a really high headboard, okay?"

"You're so pretty, Tracey. You don't have to cover up the mirror."

"That's very sweet of you, but it's so big. I don't need to see myself in tee-shirts and a robe every night."

"When Manny stops by we'll figure something out." Manny is our contractor.

When he finally arrived, Manny brought out his tape measure and began the process. "Does this seem high enough?" he asked. "It's about six feet."

"Hold on," I said. "I need to google headboards."

"I found one!" I showed Jim the picture.

"This will work."

"Seriously? What are the dimensions?"

"Eighty-four by a hundred and two."

"That's ridiculous, Tracey. A headboard that size will obliterate the entire mirror."

"Right," I nodded.

"Then what's the point of having the mirror?"

"Exactly. We should get rid of it."

"I don't want to."

"I do."

"It took willpower to keep my mouth shut."

"Let's sleep on it, okay?"

"Fine." I slapped my iPad shut. Manny retracted his tape.

We gathered our belongings and headed to the car.

"Jim, I really don't want that mirrored wall."

"We said we'd sleep on it. I don't want to argue. Let's just see how we feel about it in the morning."

Jim's musings are always reasonable. As for me, I'm myopic. It took willpower to keep my mouth shut about the mirror for the remainder of the night.

"I like where we put my desk in the bedroom," I said, beating around the bush. "The view will inspire me to write."

"That's nice, Tray." He rolled over to go to sleep.

The next morning Jim went out for coffee and returned with a gift for me. Inside was a beautiful lace nightie.

"What's this for?" I asked with a curious stare.

"A six-foot headboard," he said with a sly smile.

Stone

Last week our contractor gave us a task. "Trezzy," said Manny, with a heavy Portuguese accent, "iz time to get stoned!"

"Excuse me?" I said. "Did you say get stoned?"

"Yez," said Manny, "I'm ready for stoned."

Granted my hearing isn't great; however, that comment demanded clarification.

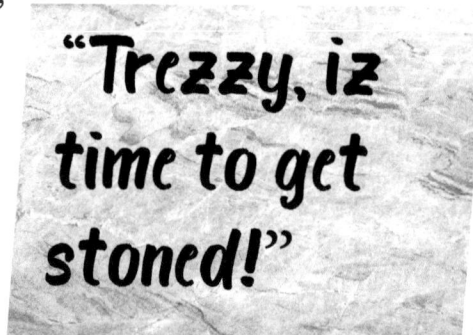

"Manny, we don't do that." I lied.

"Do what?"

"Get stoned," I said, mimicking smoking a joint.

"No Trezzy, chooz countertop for kitchen."

"Ohhhh, you mean stone like granite and marble, stuff like that."

"Yez."

"Where should we go?"

"Amazon Stone Boutique," he suggested.

"What should we look for—marble, granite, quartz or quartzite?"

"What you like?"

"Hmm."

"When you zee you knowz."

"Good advice, Manny. I hope you're right." Jim and I set out for the tile boutique, leaving Manny to continue his work.

> "Trezzy, iz time to get stoned!"

Amazon Stone was a ginormous sea of slabs with dizzying patterns and textures.

"Whoa," I said, smoothing my hand over the first slab I came to. "This is nice."

"It's marble, Tray. We're not getting marble."

"Why not?" I asked.

"Too expensive and too much upkeep."

"Fine, what do you want to look at, quartzite?"

"Yeah. Follow me."

Like Eloise at the Plaza, I brushed my hand across every stone. "This is pretty, this is pretty, this is pretty. What about this one?" Its name was Perla Venata.

"Too beige, don't ya think?" Jim opined.

"No, I see swirls of grey, white and beige running through it. I think it'll work."

I leaned my face into the polished stone. "I can see my reflection!" So naturally, I applied some lipstick.

"C'mon, be serious. Manny needs us to decide."

"What about quartz? Shouldn't we look at some of that?" I asked.

"Sure, it's over here."

When we walked through the double doors we saw a slab of Calacatta quartz. It matched my outfit perfectly.

"Twinsies." I posed next to the slab. "When you zee you knowz."

"Very funny, Tray."

We took the picture—but bought the Perla Venata.

Daughters

Cousins Molly and Nick got married last weekend, and the Fuller gals all stayed at the Courtyard by Marriott in Simi Valley. We women stick together, especially when it comes to beauty and fashion. All three of us brought 'just in cases.' That translates to 'I need choices so I'll bring everything in my closet.' Kapeesh? Here's a sneak peek into how the Fuller girls prepped for this event.

"How are you going to wear your hair tonight, girls?" I asked.

"In a bun," said Amy, "but I forgot hairspray."

"I brought spray," I said.

"Can I borrow it?" asked Amy.

"Of course."

Stephanie said she needed to wash her hair. She wanted to air dry it at the pool. "Do you want to meet me there in 30 minutes?"

"I do," I said. "But is my hair okay?"

"It looks great," said Steph.

"Then I'll go to the pool with you. But first, will you help me decide which shawl to wear?"

"What dress are you wearing?" asked Steph.

"The blue and black Lela Rose dress. The same one I forgot to bring to the last wedding."

Amy suggested I wear the black shawl and then asked us to come to her room to help her decide what to wear. Stephanie and I followed Amy to her room. She held up two outfits.

"Which one do you like better?"

"The black jumper. It's more formal." We all agreed.

When we finally got to the pool, I dozed off.

Guess what woke me up?

Five rowdy children jumped into the pool next to my lounge chair and SPLASH, my hair was soaked. "Oh, my God!" I screamed, abruptly sitting up. "That didn't just happen."

"It's okay, Mom," assured Stephanie. "Come sit next to me and let it air dry. You'll be fine."

Thank goodness for daughters, I thought. They have the uncanny ability to make everything right with the world.

"Let's take a selfie before we go girls, you both look so beautiful." 1,2,3...Smile!"

Massage

My massage therapist's fists rained down on my back. Pop. Pop. Pop. Pop. Pop. Once the pounding stopped, he thanked me and brought me a cup of cold water.

"Oh God, Tony," I said. "I can't move."

Slowly, I plunged my fingers through my tangled hair and put on my shoes. When I got home I boasted to Jim what a great massage I had.

"Did you get Tony?" he asked.

"Yesssss," I purred. "He was wonderful, but I finished my punch card. I need another one."

"Just pay as you go," said Jim. "That card cost $600."

"But I'm going tomorrow, and the card will last two seasons. I'd like another series."

"Please just pay as you go," he begged. "Don't you think you should take a day off?"

"No. I'm going tomorrow at 4 p.m."

"I have a solution." Jim brought out his Hypervolt massage device. "Bend over."

"Holy crap! Lower the speed! It's rattling my brain."

"Just relax. Let it do its work."

"How much did you pay for that thing?"

"Two fifty."

"Two hundred and fifty dollars?"

"Yeah," he said, turning off the roaring motor.

"You use it, Jim! I prefer Tony, thank you."

The next afternoon I went back to Footloose. "I'm here for a 90-minute massage with Tony. I'd like to buy a punch card, please." I handed the receptionist my credit card.

"Oh, that's not necessary, Miss Tracey," she said.

"Why not?"

"Your husband already bought card for you. He say you no like massage gun," she said in broken English.

Leave it to Jim. He always has my back.

Pin-Up Girls

My father-in-law flew a B-17 bomber for the United States Air Force. If I remember correctly, the nose of his plane had a racy pin-up girl painted on it.

After a quickie lunch in the Perez corridor, we strolled into a consignment store to look around. "Hey Jim," I said holding up a framed 8x10 picture of a pin-up girl, "didn't your dad have one of these girls painted on the nose of his airplane?"

He shuffled through a dozen or more pictures. "You know, Tray," he said, "I think he did."

"Would you recognize her?"

"I might," he said. "Why don't we buy them all and I'll see if I can find a match?"

"All twelve?" I was stunned.

"Sure, why not? Google to see if the artist is famous. They could be valuable."

I googled: 1940's pin-up artists and the name 'Elvgren,' popped up.

I held up my phone. "This is him! His name is Gil Elvgren. He shares your birthday, March 15, except he was born in 1914, a few years before you."

"We both love pin-up girls. That's my kind of guy."

I informed the consignment store owner that we would buy all 12. "I'm pretty sure one of these girls is painted on my father-in-law's World War II airplane," I told her.

"That's awesome," she said. "I'll wrap them up."

I left the store with 12 framed 1940's pin-up girls and one very happy husband. I must admit, I was intrigued, too. Wouldn't it be fun to find the one girl whose image was on dad's airplane?

When we returned home, we rummaged through a bunch of photos that dad had stuffed into a logbook of his flights.

Then, we found this "Little Gem."

Jackpot!

The Giving Plate

Last Sunday, we invited our friend Linda to come over for a juicy burger and sweet potato fries. In return, she kindly offered to bring fresh sliced watermelon.

"Thank you," I said, graciously taking the plate of watermelon from her hands. "Looks delicious."

"It's a sweet one," she said.

Jim fired up the grill. "You're the real burger king," I said, admiring his searing technique.

While the three of us chomped away at our burgers, the watermelon remained untouched.

"Don't forget to have some watermelon," said Linda, as she plucked a slice for herself.

"I won't. I love watermelon."

"I'm saving mine for desert," said Jim.

When I took a piece of watermelon, I noticed that there was a message written on the plate.

"What does the plate say, Linda? It's only partially exposed."

"You'll have to finish the watermelon to find out," she said mysteriously.

I grabbed another slice, revealing more of the message.

"C'mon, Jim. Eat up, I want to read what it says on the plate."

Finally, Jim picked up the last slice of melon and I read the message aloud.

"The Giving Plate. This plate shall have no owner for its journey will never end. It travels in a never-ending circle among our family and close friends. It brings love from home for everyone to share. The food that's placed upon it has been prepared with love and devotion. So please enjoy what is on this plate, then fill it up again and pass along the love it holds to your family and close friends."

"Friends." I looked warmly at Linda. "We picked a sweet one."

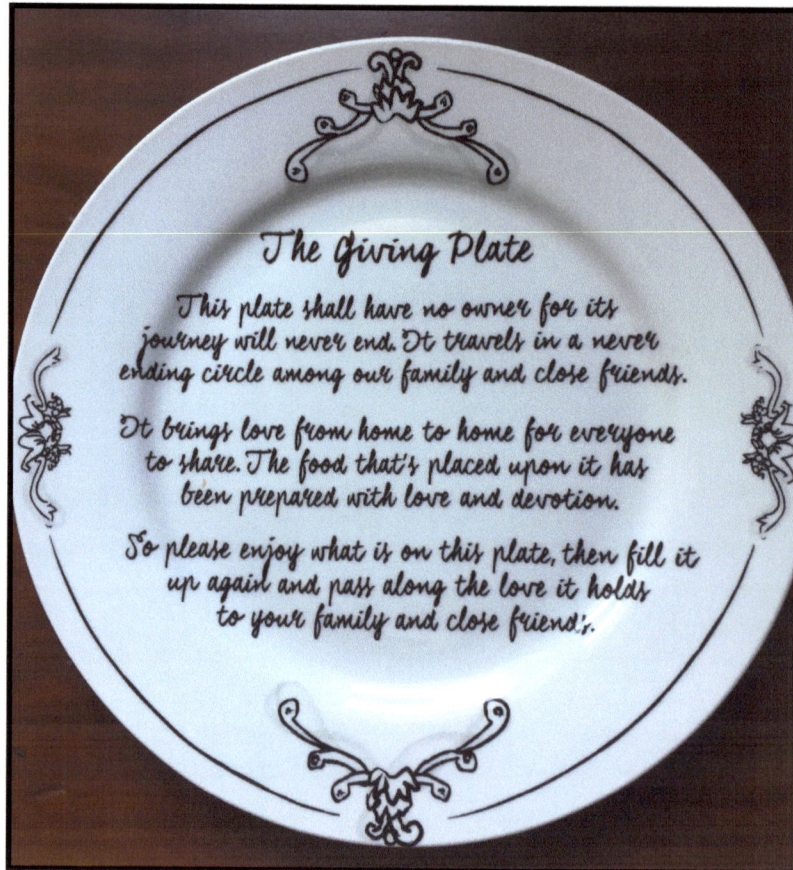

> The Giving Plate
>
> This plate shall have no owner for its journey will never end. It travels in a never ending circle among our family and close friends.
>
> It brings love from home to home for everyone to share. The food that's placed upon it has been prepared with love and devotion.
>
> So please enjoy what is on this plate, then fill it up again and pass along the love it holds to your family and close friends.

Dishwasher

Our kitchen remodel is almost finished, so now it's time to test out the appliances.

"Hey, Tray," said Jim. "Do you want to load the first set of dishes into the dishwasher, or should I?"

"You do it, okay? I'm going to hand wash the big stuff that won't fit."

"Okay, fine," he said. "But give me your opinion: should the dishes face inward or outward, and does the silverware go face-up or down?" We both eyed the complicated apparatus.

"Honey, why don't you google 'how to load a Thermador dishwasher'?"

"Very funny. I'll manage." I watched as Jim mentally calculated the machine's layout. He counted plates, bowls, etc. "I think I'll do it this way." He loaded the first dinner plate.

"Wow. That's impressive," I teased.

"Leave me alone. Don't you have other things to do?" I decided it was a good time for some tunes, so I powered up our Sonos and danced around the kitchen.

I told Jim the Cascade and Jet Dry were in the garage.

Frustrated by the task, he asked for ten minutes without interruption.

Sometime later, Jim called me over. "Check this out! There's definitely a right way and a wrong way to load dishes."

"That's amazing, Honey." I looked down with admiration at the neatly loaded dishes. "You have really mastered the art of loading a dishwasher. Let me take your picture for posterity." Jim stood above the dishwasher and smiled.

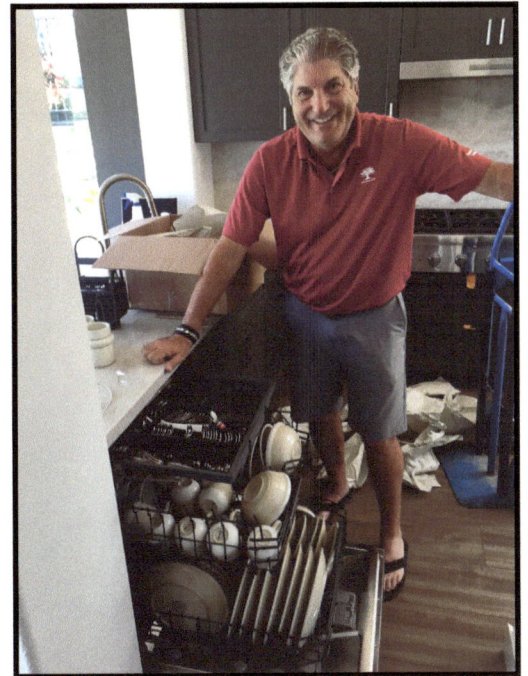

"I'll be back later, Babe." I walked out of the kitchen. "I've got to finish emptying boxes." When I returned, the dishwasher quietly hummed through the wash cycle. A digital time display reflected onto our new floors.

"They'll be done by 4:30 and clean for dinner," he said proudly, as if he had mastered a feat of engineering. Once the cycle finished, I called him over to help me unload.

When I pulled open the dishwasher, Jim blurted, "Oh shit, Tray. I forgot to put in the soap."

Treasure Hunt

The other day, I walked 3.2 miles around Batiquitos Lagoon, a coastal wetland in North San Diego County. A local legend claims there is a buried treasure on the island so I set out to find it.

Like most treasure hunters, I disguised myself in a hat and glasses. I slung a backpack over my shoulders so I could carry the buried treasure home. I told Jim about the walk, but not the hidden treasure. That would remain my secret.

"Honey," I said, "I'm going to take a walk around the lagoon, want to go?" I hoped he would say, no. He's not a believer.

"Sure," he said enthusiastically. "Can you give me an hour? I need to finish some work."

"Ugh," I sighed, then regretted asking.

"What's wrong?" he said.

"Nothing," I lied, "I'm ready to go now. Can you finish what you're doing later?"

"No, Tracey. I can't. You go."

Yes. I fist-pumped. I'm going on a treasure hunt—all by myself. I said my goodbyes and headed out the door.

At the trail entrance, I could see the vast wetland, rugged hillsides, huge palm trees, and five grazing horses. It was gorgeous. At the mile marker, I began sifting through reeds and eyeing gopher holes. Egrets flew gracefully through the air, ducks waddled around in pairs, and lizards slithered along the dirt trail. I took in all the splendid sights and sounds but kept to my mission.

Guess what I found? A cell phone partially covered in dirt. What did I do? I put it in my backpack, brought it home, located the owner, and declined a finder's fee.

Legends sure have changed these days.

Hashtag Still Looking.

Best Birthday Gift Ever

"Tracey," said Jim, "I want to do something fun with you on your birthday."

"Okay," I said, enthusiastically, "what?"

"Let's play golf at Aviara, then have dinner at the Park Hyatt."

"Sounds great. Thank you." I had a moment to ponder the plan and offered up an alternative. "Honey, I feel like I've been given so many gifts since we moved to Carlsbad, I'd like to switch it up and give you something for my birthday instead."

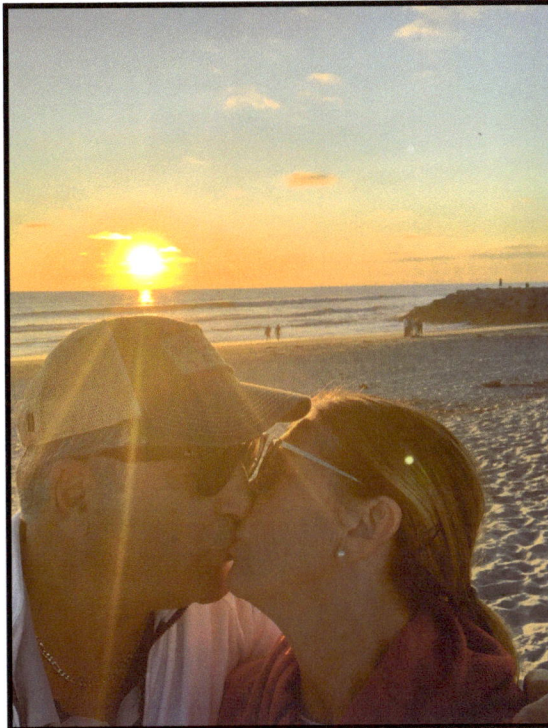

"That's not necessary, Tracey."

"But I already know where I want to take you tonight."

"Where? I don't like surprises."

"I'm not telling."

"Will you give me a clue?" he asked.

"Sure. I'm taking you to see a little orange ball."

"Miniature golfing?"

"No. Stop asking. You'll know when you know."

I put on my coziest sweater, held up my keys, and said, "Let's go!"

We took a short five-minute drive, and I parked the car on the Pacific Coast Highway.

"You're taking me to the beach?" he said, curiously.

"Uh-huh," I lifted out the chairs.

"Then why was your clue a little orange ball?"

"It's called a sunset," I pulled him in for a hug.

The moment the sun touched the horizon, I reached over for a kiss.

"Jim, thank you for sharing this beautiful life with me. Now kiss me again beneath the little orange ball."

I snapped a selfie.

Best birthday gift ever.

Reams of Eames

I bought a replica of a 1960s style Eames chair for my bedroom. It was to be my iron throne, a place to read, relax, reflect and rule my queendom.

When it arrived, I was super excited and wanted to assemble it right away. Easier said than done! It was really heavy, made in China, and came with reams of drawings that were meant to answer the question, 'how the hell do I put this thing together?'

> ## "I sat down regally on the throne-of-my own."

Historically, Jim is the assembler-in-chief. He wasn't keen on reading instructions that only consisted of illustrations. He opted to go to Vons and buy light bulbs instead. "Do you need anything?"

"But my Eames chair just arrived," I pleaded. "Don't you want to see it?"

"Not now. Manny needs bulbs to test the dining room fixture."

"But Manny isn't installing the light today. The bulbs can wait."

"I'm leaving, Tracey. I will help you assemble it when I get back." *Famous last promises.*

"Fine. Then buy me four cans of Scotchgard."

"What's that?"

"It's a fabric protector for our couch."

"I'll look for it. What aisle will it be in?"

"I don't know. Cleaning supplies, I guess."

"Okay," he said, and off he went.

There I was, with paper drawings of the Eames chair scattered about. I finally began by assembling the ottoman, which was easy enough. I was determined to have it completed by the time Jim got home. I was hoping he'd feel bad for not helping me put it together.

Miraculously, I assembled the chair all by myself. For my coronation, I poured myself a glass of wine and sat down regally on the throne-of-my-own.

I awaited Jim's arrival, anticipating his guilt for abandoning me in my time of need.

"Honey, come into our bedroom." I raised my glass of wine. "Notice anything?"

"Sorry, Tray," he said, not recognizing that I was in the new chair. "I forgot the Scotchgard."

We Got One

A sunrise met my eyes on the morning of my sixty-second birthday. Jim and I were on the boardwalk in Newport Beach, lifeguard tower six. We were guests at the Barnett's beach house.

"Good morning," I said to Debbie as she emerged from the house.

"How'd ya sleep?" she asked.

"Great! I woke up at sunrise to begin celebrating sixty-two."

"Happy Birthday!"

"Thanks, Deb. I keep thinking of all the years we've spent on this beach with our kids. They were simply the best."

"So true," she said. "Now that they are all adults, getting them here is a challenge."

Just then I received a text from my daughter Stephanie: Happy Birthday, Ma! What is the address in Newport?

Are you coming here? I replied.

Yup.

"Debbie, we got one! Stephanie's coming to Newport."

"That's great! Tell her to park on Island."

I texted Stephanie the address, then Debbie and I walked to the water's edge.

"Cheers to thirty-some-odd years on this beach, in these chairs, and at this house," I said, holding up my bottle of water.

We toasted, shared stories, took naps, and slowly made our way back to the house.

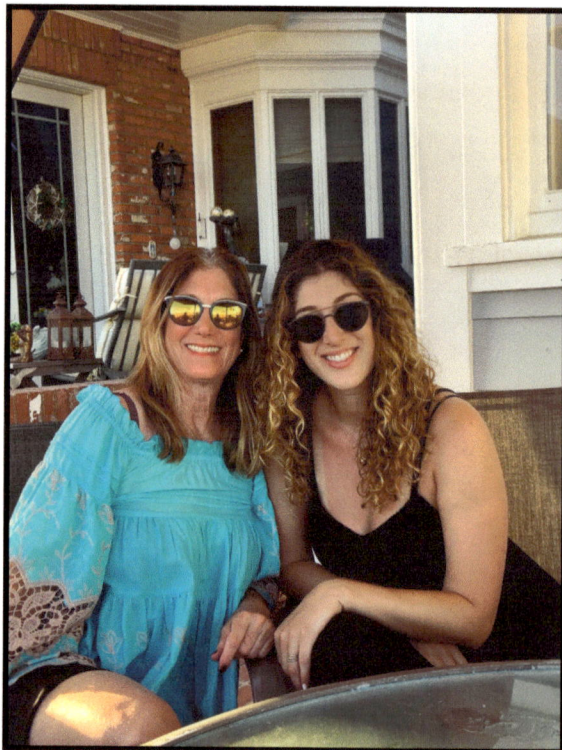

"Hiya Ma!" said Stephanie, arriving at cocktail hour, "Happy Birthday."

"Thank you, Honey." I leaned in for a hug. "Seeing you is the best gift any mom could wish for."

Stephanie sat down beside me and smiled as Debbie captured the moment.

Debbie flashed a thumbs-up. "We got one!"

Me and My Gals

Jim was away on a guys' trip, so naturally, I decided to go on a girls' trip. The only girls I wanted to see were my own, Amy and Stephanie. But Amy was in Denver, and Stephanie had recently moved into a duplex in Los Angeles. Despite it all, the girls and I developed a plan—I would help Stephanie organize her new place, and Amy would fly to Cali for a weekend. Mom's perfect scenario. Here is a peek into the lives and loves of mothers and daughters.

"Ma," said Stephanie, "my new place does not have a built-in closet so I bought a Rubbermaid 'do-it-yourself' kit. Will you help me put it together? Lewis is away on a business trip."

"Of course I will. But do you have a handyman in case the project is more than we can handle?"

"No, Ma, I don't." She paused. "Or maybe I do! Task Rabbit."

"Can the rabbit drill holes and build closets? Because if he can, hire him, please."

Stephanie arranged for the rabbit to assist us and we carried on with our tasks; bathroom fixtures, T.V set up, area rugs, curtains, and art." Through it all, we sweated, laughed, and beautified her new apartment. Each night we fell into bed exhausted, well-fed, and happy.

On my last day with Stephanie, our goodbye hug lingered. "Thanks for everything, Mom. I love you so much." I could not hold back my tears. It was so hard to leave her.

Amy arrived late Friday afternoon and we spent all day and night talking about everything that popped into our heads. Saturday, we had a massage at the Park Hyatt and lunch by the pool. Amy's friend Emily came by for a cocktail then we feasted on pheasant and sea bass at Paon in the Village.

On my last day with Amy, we strolled the Carlsbad boardwalk. "Let's take a selfie," I said, while waves pounded the jetty.

Our goodbye hug lingered. "Thanks for everything, Mom. I love you so much." I could not hold back my tears. It was so hard to watch her leave.

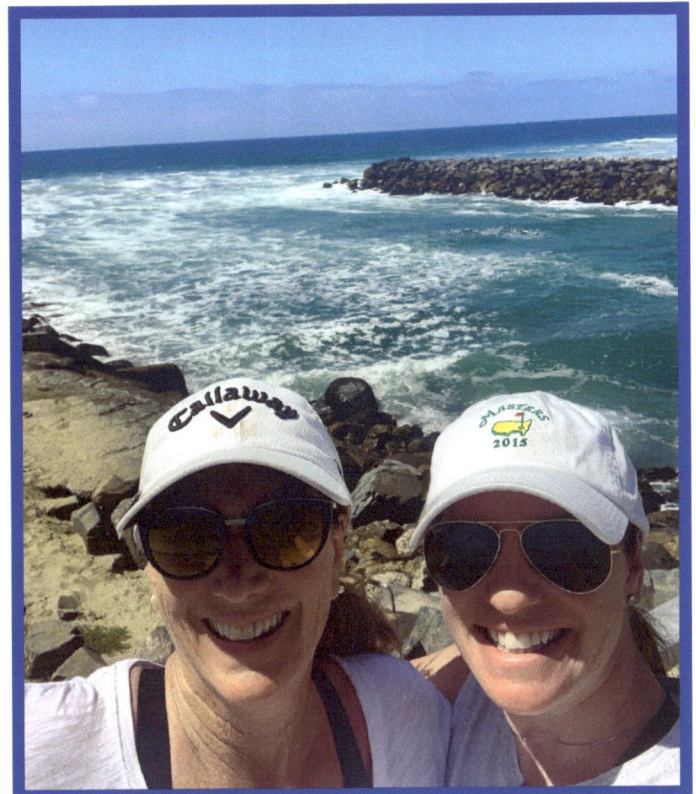

Distractions

Every week I set aside time to write my banana stories, but housework distracts me. It's not an urge to fluff pillows, but if I see a scuff mark, I'm on it.

"Jim, your golf shoes are leaving scuff marks on the floor."

"I doubt it, Tray," he said, grabbing a power bar. "Check yours."

"Nope. I'm wearing slippers."

"What do you want me to do? I'm going to the golf course now."

"Goodbye. I'll see you later," I said, aggravated.

I sat down at my computer and typed *I Don't Have Time for my Husband's Golf Shoes.* Oops, delete.

Draped over my chair were three dirty bras. Gotta wash those, I thought. Since my hands were already wrinkled from washing the bras, I decided to take a shower. Unfortunately, I scratched a tile with my squeegee. Frustrated, I went back to my computer and typed *I Don't Have Time for Dirty Bras or Tiles.* Oops, delete. That's when I heard Jim come home. "Take off your shoes!" I yelled.

"I gotta pee," he announced," rushing past me to the bathroom.

When he came out, he asked, "Where's my toothbrush, Tracey?"

"I used it to clean off your scuff marks."

"Why *my* toothbrush?" he asked.

"Because I've been distracted all morning. I was trying to write a banana story, but the marks from your shoes bugged me. So, I grabbed your toothbrush to clean the floor."

"Why didn't you grab yours?"

"Because they were *your* scuff marks, so it had to be *your* toothbrush."

"It was barely used," he frowned.

"Sorry, I have to confess—our squeegee scratched the tile in the shower. Your toothbrush came in handy for that, too."

"Swell."

"Look, I don't have time to visit now. I need to write a story for next week."

"Fine. Go."

I went back to my writing desk and closed the door. Guess what I typed? *I Don't Have Time for Green Bananas or Anything Else.* Oops, delete.

I took a nap.

Cinépolis

"Hey Tray," said Jim, "let's go see *Brittany Runs a Marathon* at Cinépolis."

"What the hell is that?"

"I don't know, but *Downton Abbey* is sold out."

"Have you read a review?"

"No," he admitted. "But it's rated 90% on the Tomatometer."

"That's swell if you're garlic," I jested. "Okay, I'll go for the popcorn and Red Vines."

The Cinépolis theater was so luxurious we felt like we were transported to Highclere Castle in Downton Abbey. The lobby furnishings consisted of oversized upholstered couches, tufted chairs, and tulip tables.

"Wow, this place is gorgeous. Check out the crystal chandeliers."

"Want a drink?" asked Jim, standing at the bar.

"Yes, I do. But where are the Red Vines and popcorn?"

The bartender answered, "There is a menu at your seat. Theater Two."

"Oh, my God!" I said, wandering the aisles. "Check out the leather chairs with tray tables and lamps. We're the only ones here."

"Let me escort you to your seat, My Lady," said Jim, in his best British accent.

"Have a seat, Your Lordship."

"Wine, My Lady?"

"Are you sure we're not here to see *Downton Abbey*?" I asked.

"Nope. We're going to see *Brittany Runs a Marathon*."

"Oh, Lord," I shrugged. "Let's eat."

"What would you like?"

"I fancy wine, potstickers, popcorn, and Red Vines." Jim pushed the call button to alert our server. *Lights fade. Curtain up. Showtime.* The room was dimly lit, but I could cheerfully see our handsome waiter.

"What can I get you?" he said, bending low to assure our view was unobstructed. Jim rattled off our order.

I gave our waiter a flirtatious smile and said, "Thank you, Mr. Carson."

When the Cat's Away

Jim was going to San Francisco on a business trip for a night. His absence afforded me an opportunity to accomplish a task.

"Hey Jim," I said. "What time are you leaving tomorrow?"

"Why? You gonna miss me?"

"No. I mean yes," I corrected, "but I'm happy for you. Can I help you put stuff in the car?"

"Are you plotting something—because it feels like you're rushing me out of the house."

"No, no. no," I defended, "I thought you might want help."

Truth be told, I intended to paint my living room wall while Jim was out of town.

"That's comforting," he said, "because you're acting strange. Are you going to the gym this morning?"

"Yes, but I won't be leaving before you."

Meanwhile, I studied the wall that I intended to paint and thought, this might be too hard for me. I can't move the couch or the coffee table. If I ask Jim for help he'll know what I am up to.

Instead, I texted our contractor: Good morning Manny. Can you help me paint the living room wall today? Shhh, don't tell Jim, it's a surprise. Then I hit send.

"I made your favorite eggs," I said. "I thought I'd send you off with a full belly."

"That's nice, Tracey. What's this?" Jim showed me his phone.

Embarrassed, I read the text: Good morning Manny. Can you help me paint the living room wall today? Shhh, don't tell Jim, it's a surprise.

I grabbed Jim's phone. "I was going to surprise you."

"You sure as shit did, Tray."

"When the cat's away." I said, caught like a deer in headlights.

Jim kissed me goodbye, and Manny never came to help.

The wall remains white.

114

Full House

Renovating your home is a gamble unto itself. You are at the mercy of contractors; supply chains are slow, and everything is very expensive. So, a little negotiating with my husband became part of our routine. Here's one example.

"Jim," I said, "I want a Toto washlet toilet in our master bathroom."

"What the hell is that?"

"It's like a bidet and toilet in one. I've heard they are life-altering."

"Tracey, I've lived 65 years without one. That's not a sound argument."

"But you *need* one."

"They cost a fortune, don't they?"

"Not if you consider the cost of underwear."

"Ha-ha, Tray. How much?"

"Around $1,500," I mumbled. "But..."

Jim cut me off. "No! I'm not paying $1,500 for a toilet."

"It has a remote," I said, raising my eyebrows. "You love remotes."

"What for?"

"There are too many features for me to describe, but you can figure out the important ones, can't you?"

"Yes, Tracey. I know what a bidet does."

"Then promise me you'll keep an open mind."

"Fine. But don't count on it."

I let the toilet topic go for a few days but brought it up again at cocktail hour. "Let's make a wager." I walked over to our Draw Poker machine. "If I pull a straight flush, you'll buy me the toilet."

"Okay," he laughed. "You're on."

I pulled a pair of tens and one five. Then I renegotiated. "A straight flush appears to be impossible at this point, so let's change the bet from a straight flush to a full-house, okay? I only have one pull left." Jim looked at me, then studied the odds on the machine. "Okay, Tracey, I'll make that bet."

Guess who won?

Let's just say, if you ever use our bathroom, you'll be enjoying your own 'royal flush!'

Three P's

When you go to your parents' house for the weekend, you are unlikely to pack shampoo and toothpaste, knowing that those items are readily available. I get that. But packing in general is synonymous with forgetfulness. Inevitably, you forget to pack something you need.

Before we left for Carlsbad last week, Jim and I engaged in our typical pre-departure conversation.

"Do you have your pills, pillow, and plugs, Jim?" P1, P2, & P3.

"Yes, Tracey, why do you always ask me that?"

"Because you always forget one or all three, that's why."

When Jim brings a pillow, he forgets to take it home. If he uses one he likes, he'll take it home thinking it's his.

Before my cousin Susie came to visit us in Carlsbad, I told her to pack her creature comforts because I may not have exactly what she needs.

Susan arrived and departed with her pillow.

"Did you notice that SuSu brought her own pillow?" I informed Jim.

"Yes. So?"

"She remembered to take it home, too."

"Is that a jab?"

"Yes, if the shoe fits."

Before my kids came to visit, I reminded them to bring *their* creature comforts too. Here's how that went.

Arrival Day. "Ma," said Steph, "I forgot to pack my allergy pills. Do you have any?" P1

Departure Day Text. Ma, I can't find my pajamas and Lewis left his iPhone plug on the bedside table. P2, P3

I texted her back. I've got your stuff.

Just keep them in a drawer, she replied. We'll get them next time.

The following day Steph phoned again to tell me she misplaced her sunglasses. Sunglasses don't fit the *P-mold*, but whatever. S1.

Found them!

You can keep them, she replied. They'll look cute on you. She was right. I wore them every day.

Pam and Steve were in route for a weekend visit when a text came in from Pam: I left my iPhone plug at home. Do you have an extra? P1

"Yes," I answered, "several." And so, the story goes...

Rise and Shine

Seven houseguests in a month was a bit ambitious. But we were so excited to share Carlsbad with our family and friends. "It's great when they come and it's great when they go," I said to Jim, reminiscing over each visit. I was exhausted.

"Next time we have visitors, let's try new places."

"But I love hiking Batiquitos Lagoon and Torrey Pines State Park."

"I know," he said. "I'm talking about restaurants. We always go to Black Rail and the Park Hyatt. We should switch it up next time."

"You are all about the food, aren't you, Jim?"

"Yes, I am," he agreed. "But I think our friends would love the pancake house in Bressi Ranch and Saint Archers in Encinitas."

"What about hiking? Personally, I'd rather hike than eat."

"We have to eat, Tray."

"I'm so tired, Jim," I said. "Can we discuss this later. I need a nap."

I lay down on the couch and fell asleep. An hour later, "Rise and shine. You don't want to miss this sunset."

I felt a nudge. "Not now," I whispered.

Jim persisted. "Wake up, Tracey."

When I opened my eyes, I saw the horizon streaked with hues of orange, purple and red. "Babe," I sighed. "It's beautiful, but I was in the middle of a great dream."

"What were you dreaming about?"

"I was devouring a Double-Double from In-N-Out Burger."

"You were eating?"

"Yes, but I had just finished a long, grueling hike."

"Sure you did," he said sarcastically.

I sat up taller this time and gazed out at the beautiful sunset.

"Gary and Ann-Marie are coming next Sunday," said Jim.

"Fantastic! But right now, I'm starving. What's for dinner?"

Jim nudged me on the shoulder and said, "Take a hike!"

Stretch

For months now, I have driven past a place called, Stretch Zone. They advertise, "FLEX-ABILITY for LIFE." I wanted that, so I decided to drop in.

While I waited for Victoria, the receptionist, I eyed a bowl of individually wrapped Life-savers. Candy always draws my attention. It's a sign, I thought. Stretching is a Life-Saver. I wondered if that's why they served that candy. Yum. I ate two.

"Hi, Tracey," said a fit young woman. "I'm Taylor. Would you like a free thirty-minute stretch at your convenience."

"Now?" I said, hopefully, aching all over.

"No," said Taylor, but I am available next Monday at three. Are you?"

"Yes, yes, yes," I groaned. "I am."

The following Monday, Taylor strapped various parts of my body to the table and tested my "flex-ability." I didn't have much.

"Are you stretching at home?" she asked, pulling my leg to the edge of discomfort."

"Not enough to do any good." Taylor was gentle in her technique, and I was a cautious participant. "Oh, my God. This hurts so good."

"I'm glad you like it, Tracey." She helped me up at the end of our 30 minutes.

"I'd like a dozen sessions, please. I'll use six and give my husband six."

"That would be awesome," she said. "Does your husband stretch at home?"

"Only in the seventh inning." Wink. Wink.

"No, really," she said, "I'll give you some stretching exercises to do together. Do you think he'll do them?"

"I doubt it," I grumbled. "That's WAY too much of a stretch!"

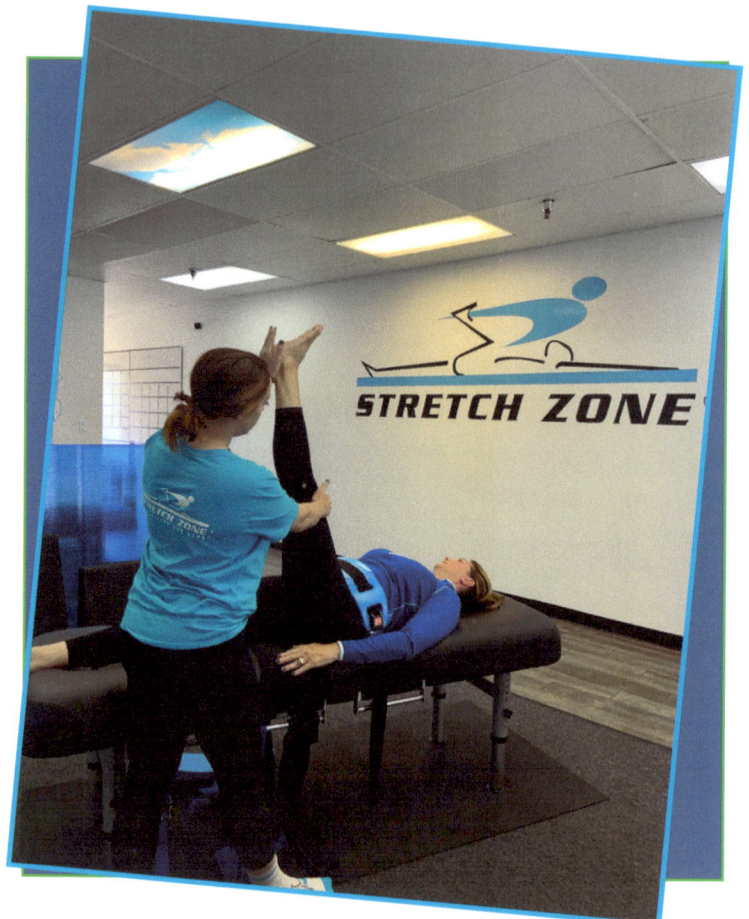

Stress the Dress

I loathe shopping for clothes, especially formal ones, so to calm myself down I talk to my husband.

"Jim, I keep getting phone notices that say I'm spending a third of my time searching for gala dresses."

"How does it know you're searching for dresses?"

"*It* doesn't. *I* do!"

"So stop searching online and go to Nordstrom's."

"Easy for you to say. But shopping makes me ill."

"That's absurd," he said.

I googled: Does shopping make some people physically ill?

I found 90,200,000 results, all referring to shopping addicts.

I'm not an addict, I thought. I'm the opposite.

So, I googled: What is the opposite of addict?

That's when I found the word, *Sane.* It read: the opposite of addict is, NOUN, sane person.

"See, Jim?" I showed him my phone. "I'm not crazy when I say shopping makes me sick. In fact, I googled it and it says I'm a sane person."

"You're nuts, Tray. Turn off your phone and go shopping."

Jim watched as I backed my car out of the garage, then stopped abruptly.

"What's wrong? Aren't you going shopping?"

"Yeah, yeah," I lied. "I'm going to call my sister first."

He retreated into the house and closed the garage door.

"Kathy," I said, "do you have a gala dress that I can borrow?"

"Absolutely!" she answered.

Decision made. I'll wear my sister's.

Fitting

Somehow, I managed to pick the right guy, so why the hell can't I pick the right bra?

In my twenties, I bought sexy bras. In my thirties, nursing bras. Forties, sports bras.

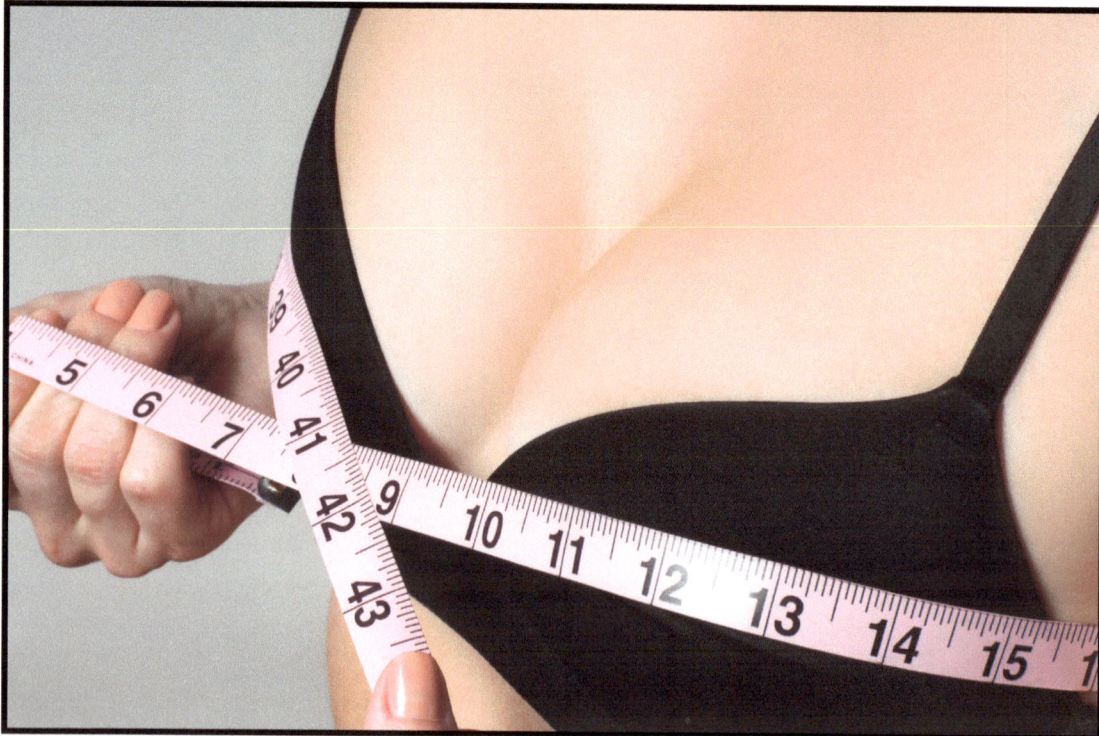

Fifties, padded. Sixties, who knows?

One thing I know for sure, the moment I get home I whip that sucker off. Then, I give a little scratch and sigh from the sheer relief of it all.

"Welcome to Soma," said a saleslady. "Is there anything I can help you find?"

"As a matter of fact, yes, I need bras."

"We have several options for you," she said, waving her arm around like Vanna White. "What size?"

"Hmm." I looked down at my chest.

"Would you like me to measure you?"

"I guess so."

"When were you last professionally measured?"

"When I was twelve," I jested.

"What's your name?" she asked.

"Tracey."

"So is mine! I spell it with an 'I.'"

"I'm an EY."

"Follow me," she said.

Once in the dressing room, I stripped down to a white tee-shirt and jeans.

"Should I take off my tee shirt?"

"No. You're fine. Sorry, my hands are cold."

She wrapped a measuring tape around my chest then said, "You're a size (not telling).

120

Later that evening I modeled for him, wearing only "Stunning" and a pair of skinny jeans.

I'll bring in some bras for you to try."

A few minutes later. Knock. Knock.

"Come in," I said.

"Try these," she instructed. "They're our top sellers."

"Thank you, Traci." The bras she handed me had names; Sensuous, Stunning and Embraceable.

Wow! I thought. I want to be all those things. I held up Stunning then tried it on. This is pretty, I thought. Then I tried on Sensuous and Embraceable. "Yeah baby," I said, feeling sexy in my new bras. "I feel like twenty all over again."

Knock. Knock.

"How ya doin'?" Traci called out over the dressing room door.

"I'll take them all."

"Really? They all fit?"

"Yes! I'm going to wear Stunning home." Traci cut off the tags and sent me on my way. I couldn't wait to show Jim.

Later that evening I modeled for him, wearing only Stunning and a pair of skinny jeans.

"Notice anything different?" I struck a pose.

"Yeah, Tray. You cut your hair."

He's still the right guy.

He just gets things wrong occasionally.

Back Scratch

"Honey," I said, "will you scratch my back?"

Jim glided his fingernails across my back.

"Harder," I demanded. "I'm so itchy."

He dug a little deeper.

"A little to the right. Up. Left. Softer. Harder," I instructed.

"Hey Tray. I've scratched three words into your skin."

"What?"

"*I am done.*" He enunciated each word slowly.

"Noooo," I begged. "There's no one else to scratch my back but you."

"Tracey, do you remember how to play 'guess what letter this is?'"

"Are you messing with me? Because my itchy back is no laughing matter. I can't do it myself, ya know."

"No. I'm serious."

I wrapped my arms around his body. "Scratch my back where I scratch yours."

"Fine." He gave in to my desires.

"Doesn't that feel good?" I asked.

"Not really. My back doesn't itch."

"You're mean."

"Turn around. I'll take care of this once and for all. Instead of scratching your back, I'll give you a massage."

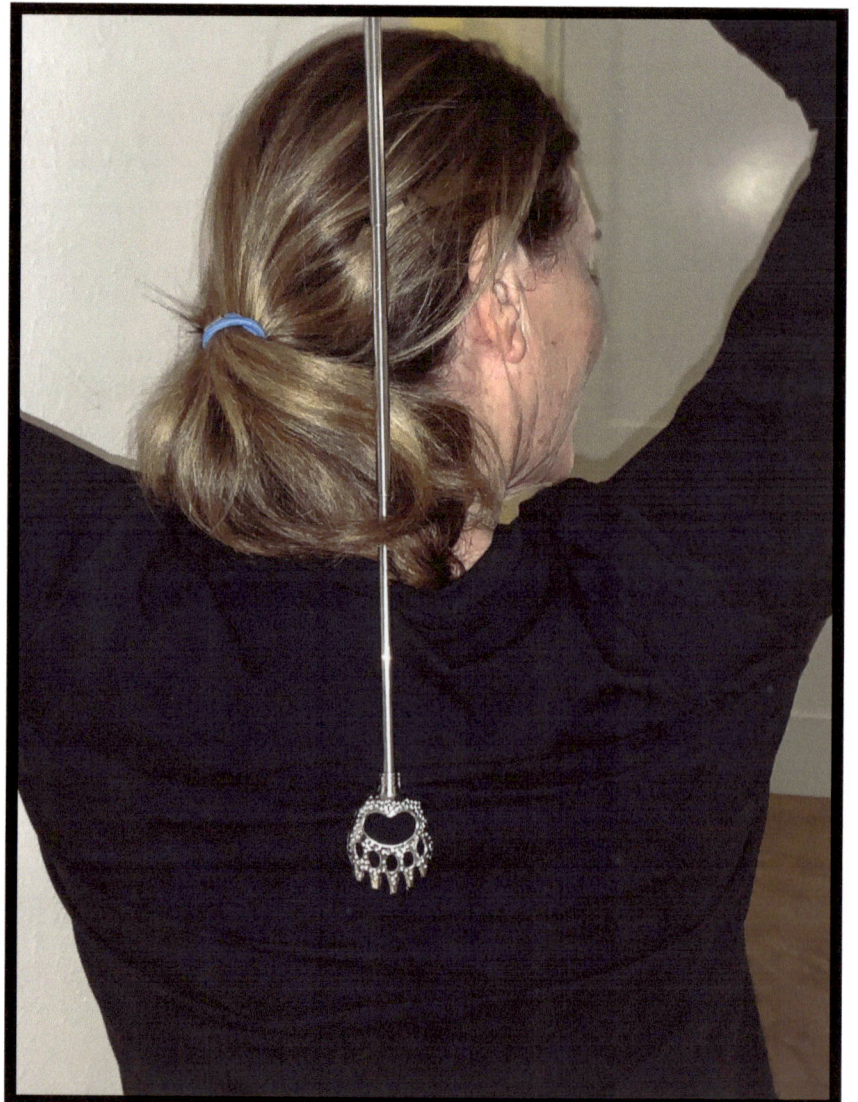

"That's a deal." After drizzling my back with oil, Jim began a gentle massage. "What a great idea."

"Thank you."

"Could you press a little harder, please?"

"Tracey, can you just be quiet and enjoy the massage?"

"I'm trying, but..."

"But what?" he asked, miffed.

"I'm still itchy."

Jim grabbed his phone.

"No more?" I said, wishing I hadn't sounded so ungrateful.

"No more. I just bought you a back scratcher on Amazon instead. It will arrive in 24 hours."

Next time, I'll keep quiet.

"There's no one else to scratch my back but you."

Mr. Sloppy

I always like to prepare meals for Thanksgiving week, but every time I do, the kids don't want what to eat what I've made and that makes me mad. For instance, I made a savory frittata filled with veggies and all they wanted were scrambled eggs and toast. News Flash kids: Frittatas *are* eggs. I discussed this with Jim before the entourage came to town.

"What should I do about feeding the kids for the holiday? I'm feeling overwhelmed."

"Don't do anything. Let things flow naturally."

"It doesn't work that way, Jim. We'll have a house full of hungry adults and we need three meals a day."

"You take charge of Thanksgiving; the kids can fend for themselves the rest of the time."

"No," I argued. "I don't like that answer. I have fed these girls for thirty some odd years. It's my job. I want to plan for nice lunches and dinners, especially for when the leftovers are gone."

"You're your own worst enemy. You can't be mad at the kids if they want to choose their own food. My suggestion is don't make the frittata this time. It's getting old."

"*Old?* The frittata is *not* getting old. *I* am!"

"No, you're not," he said, curbing my frustration. "Think of it this way, Tracey—when the kids prepare their own meals, you get to relax."

"Okay fine," I compromised. "I won't make a frittata."

"Good," he nodded. "Are we done?"

"No," I persisted. "What about lunch before our Thanksgiving feast? I would like to prepare something easy that everyone will eat and a dish that I can prepare ahead of time.

"Like what?"

"I don't know. That's why I'm asking you. But I want it to be clean and easy."

"Most people like sandwiches for lunch. Just buy some ham and cheese."

"No way! I want something more festive."

"Whatever, Tray," he shrugged. "I'm over it." Jim walked away.

"C'mon," I whined. "It's going to rain both days and we'll be trapped inside the house.

Not to mention, the fridge is so stuffed, I don't have room for another thing."

"*Old?* The frittata is *not* getting old. *I* am!"

Jim pulled out his phone. He searched for a recipe for Thanksgiving lunch. "Give me a few minutes," he said as he scrolled. "I got it! The perfect lunch. Everyone will love them."

"What?" I asked, wary of what he was about to say.

"Sloppy Joes."

"Those aren't clean—they're sloppy!"

"But they're *easy*!"

Card Game

It was a rainy Thanksgiving Day and football games were blaring out of the TV. "Where's the flag, Ref?" said Jim.

"That's a fumble!" shouted Lew.

"How did he miss that kick?" said Jason.

"He was down!" roared Amy.

I had a room full of sports announcers shouting expletives in surround-sound. At some point, (who knows when) a game ended. The room was dead silent. "Is football over?" I asked.

"No way, Tray," said Jason. "The Bills and Cowboys are coming up." I shrugged. My son-in-law picked up on my mood.

"Wanna learn a new card game?" Jason announced. "We can play and watch the game at the same time."

"Yes," I said, quickly. "All of us?"

"Of course," he answered.

I scanned the lazy faces around the room hoping to gain a consensus. Everyone agreed to play cards. We took our seats at the dining room table. I was extra thirsty after eating the Sloppy Joes so I offered everyone chilled cans of White Claw.

"I love those, Ma," said Stephanie. "And, they give you a slight buzz."

"I could use a little buzz right now," I said. So, I popped open a couple cans and sat down to play cards.

"The object of the game," said Jason, "is to get rid of all of your cards. The person left with cards, in the end, is an asshole."

"Excuse me. What?" I said, staring at my son-in-law.

"Sorry, Tray. The game is called Asshole."

"Is it like Bullshit?"

"No," said Jason. "Here's why." Jason rambled off the rules of the game ending with this: "The President begins the game with the first turn, followed by the Vice President, then the middle of the pack, and finally the Vice-Asshole and Asshole."

"Sounds like, Make Cards Great Again," I joked.

By round three, I was the only one left holding a card.

The queen of hearts.

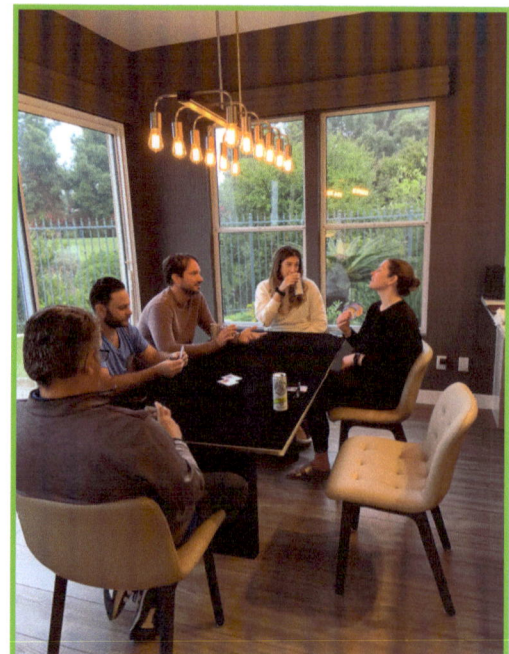

Goodwill

"I'm donating a bunch of stuff to Goodwill," I said to Jim during the Pittsburgh v. New England football game.

"Great!" he said. "While you're there, buy me an ugly Christmas sweater for the party next week."

"Don't you have one?"

"No," he argued. "You gave it to Goodwill last year."

"I did?"

"Yeah. You purge stuff every year."

"No, I don't!" I shrieked. "What did it look like?"

"It was my burgundy Happy Elfin' holiday sweater."

"That was cute on you," I admitted. "But I don't remember giving it away. Will you check all your drawers, first?"

"I'll get to it," he said, paying little attention. Volume up.

"Right," I murmured. That's code for *never*. As I rummaged through drawers and cabinets for items to take to Goodwill, I stumbled upon an Asian elephant box that had a hidden drawer. I opened the drawer.

"Oh, my God! I found the missing key to the marble top chest in the entryway."

"Lemme see," he demanded. I handed him the key. It had been missing for a year, and the contents of the chest were a mystery. Jim paused the football game. "Who put it in there?"

"I don't know, but if I hadn't been purging our tchotchkes, I never would have found it. Go try the key."

Look what he found.

What A Moment

There are many moments in life worth re-membering. Some stand out above all others. This was one of those moments.

"Honey," I said, "we are alone this Christmas."

"I know, Tracey, but at least we have each other." Jim put a loving arm around my shoulder. I nestled my head into his chest.

"I want to cry," I sighed.

"We knew this day would come," he said, trying to comfort me. "I fully expected the girls would spend the holidays with their in-laws and that they'd be away at the same time. We had them for Thanksgiving. Don't be sad. We'll plan to do some fun things."

"Like what?" I mumbled.

"We'll hang out with friends, go to a fancy Christmas Eve dinner, and watch Elf."

"I'll cook a traditional Hanukkah dinner, too."

"Brisket?" asked Jim, excited.

"Latkes, too. By the way, are we planning to exchange presents?"

"I'll tell you what, Tray. We just purged a houseful of tchotchkes, so we definitely don't want more of those."

"That's true," I agreed. "So we're not exchanging presents, right?"

"C'mere," he said, luring me back into his arms. "I want to take you somewhere."

"Where?" I said, curiously.

"It's a surprise," he said. "Go get a jacket."

I pulled out a scarf and jacket from my closet then followed Jim to the car.

He drove me ten minutes away to Ponto beach. We parked and walked to the edge of the moat. Pensively, we stood beside one another gazing at the breathtaking skyline.

"It's so beautiful here." I was mesmerized by the hugeness of the ocean.

"Mommy, Mommy," said a child nearby. "Look!"

Behind us, a woman was playing in the sand with her young daughter.

Jim turned around. "Hi," he said to the woman. "Would you mind taking a picture of me and my wife?"

"Sure," she said. "No problem."

He handed her his phone and continued their conversation. "Our kids are away for the holiday. My wife is kind of sad.

But we're here together and she's all I need."

"That's so sweet," said the woman. "I'd be happy to take your picture. My name is Brandi. This is Victoria. Merry Christmas!"

"Take my hand, Tracey."

Brandi trailed beside us clicking photos. "I got a few good ones," she said.

The coastline was ours alone. The clouds were mysterious, the air cool.

Suddenly, Jim stopped and cradled my face in the palms of his hands.

"Tracey." He lookied deep into my eyes. "You are the only present that I will ever want or need."

What a moment.

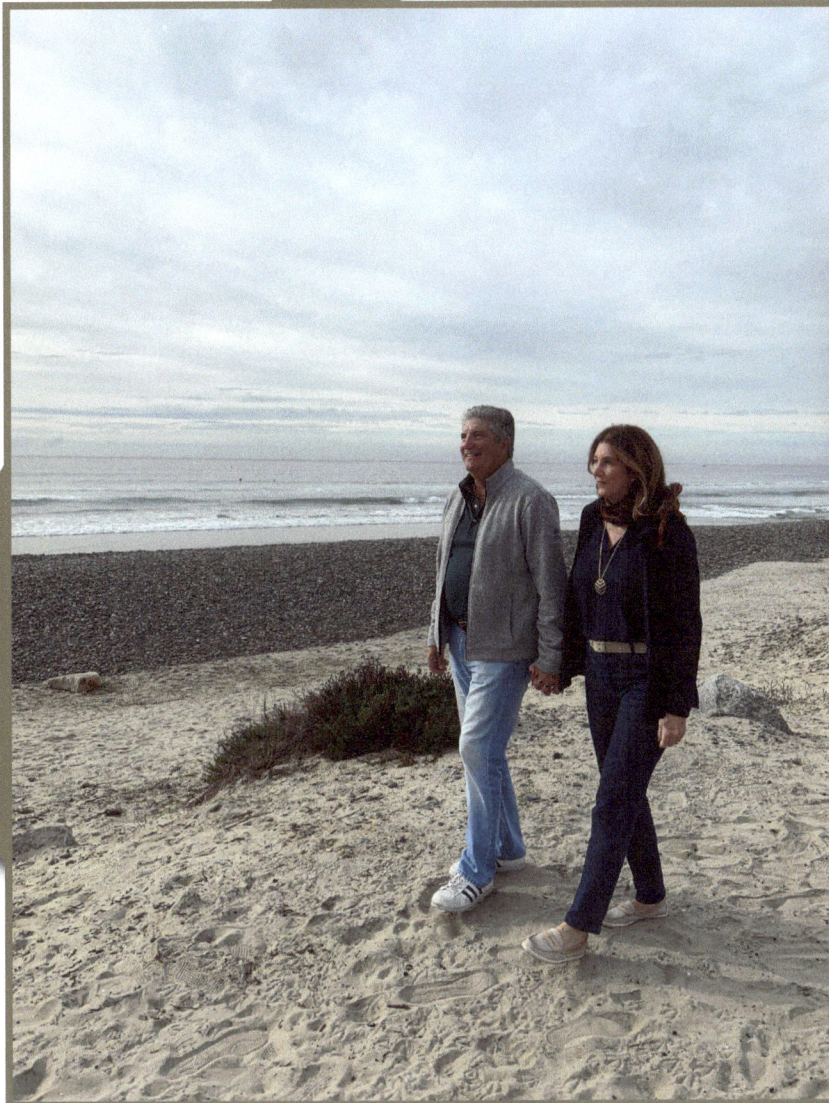

Monday Hug

"Are you feeling okay today, Tray?" asked Jim, a day after the new year began.

I could barely speak. My lungs constricted, body ached.

"No," I sighed. "I'm sick."

I loved having him home.

Jim, as is his nature, gave me a hug. A Thursday hug.

"I'll get you some Tylenol. Then you can rest. I'm playing golf today. Will you be okay alone?"

"Yes, Honey. I'll sleep."

With my face buried in my pillow, I wheezed myself to sleep. Two hours later I awoke. I'll have some soup, I thought.

Pantry contents; canned tomatoes, olives and stone ground mustard.

"Ick," I murmured. "Now what?"

I put on some sweats and drove to the market. Two hours later I had an enormous pot of vegetable soup. Admittedly, I cut corners. I used frozen veggies alongside fresh, but no mind, the soup was simmering and delicious. It was day one of my 5:2 diet, and only protein and veggies were allotted for consumption that day. I gobbled up a bowl of soup then retreated to bed.

Jim returned from golf. I felt a kiss on my forehead and woke up.

"Hi," I said groggily. "How was golf?"

"I lost. Girard beat me by a stroke."

"Oh well," I shrugged, "it's only a game."

"I know."

Jim lounged in our bedroom chair and quietly kept me company. I loved having him home.

Friday morning my head throbbed. I clasped my hands over my face and began to weep.

Jim noticed my wet cheeks. "I'll get you a warm washcloth. That always seems to help."

I couldn't speak. I could only moan. I held the warm towel over my face. "Ah," I sighed. "Thank you."

Day three, always the worst, lived up to its promise. But I had a plan to lift my spirits. I watched Funny Girl.

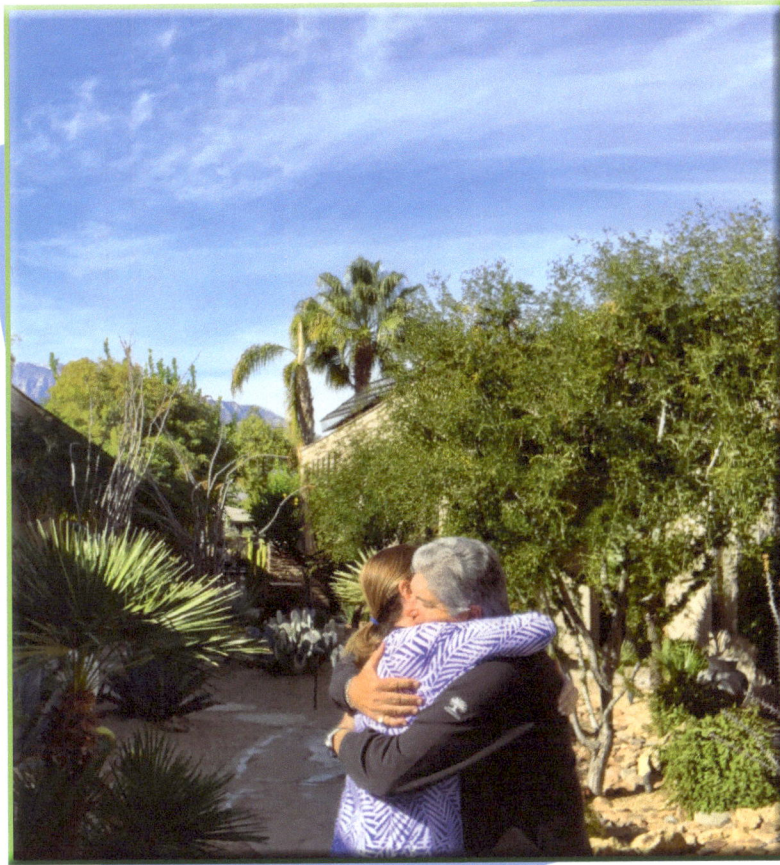

Imagine this—sick me, sitting up in bed mimicking Barbra Streisand. *"I'm a nach'ral cougher. Ah hee, ah who, ah hee."*

Two hours later, I sat in the yard and let the sun do its magic. Wearing a large brimmed hat and sunglasses, I continued my Funny Girl high. I began to lip-sync, *"Lookin' down you'll never see me—try the sky, 'cause that'll be me..."*

My arms gestured, my chest lifted my spirits rose.

"In all of the world so far, I'm the greatest star!"

Saturday night Jim went to the deli and brought me home some matzo ball soup. Sunday, we watched football and the Golden Globes. Nothing like glamorous star distractions to kickstart the week.

In the kitchen Monday morning, while I prepared my first cup of Matcha in four days Jim looked at me with outstretched arms and said, "You haven't had your Monday hug, yet."

I fell into his comforting embrace.

"Have you guessed yet,

Who's the best yet?"

Grateful.

2020

"I've got an idea," I said to Jim the other day.

"Uh-oh. What?"

"Why don't we try something new in 2020?"

"What are you cookin' up now?"

"I'm not going to be cooking anything in 2020."

"C'mon. What are you talking about?"

"I don't want to cook anymore. You cook."

"Are you serious?"

"Yes."

"Can we discuss this later?" Jim stood up.

"No. Please hear me out." I reminded Jim that I've cooked for him for 36 years and I'm fresh out of ideas.

"What's really bugging you, Tracey?"

"I want a sous chef. Cooking takes too long. I saw a show about intermittent fasting. Let's do that. Eat five days, fast two."

"I'll fast with you occasionally," said Jim. "That's not a problem."

"You will?"

"I'll try. But what about cooking?" He sounded a little concerned.

"I guess I'll still cook for us," I reassured him.

"Phew!" He wiped his brow.

"But only on the days that we fast."

From my family to yours...Happy 2020!

132

A Tribute to Nathan O. Reynolds

I attended Westlake School for Girls in 1974 and 1975. I graduated, thanks to passing senior English taught by our brilliant headmaster, Nathan O. Reynolds.

"Girls," he said, "you will be writing one book report while in my class."

"Only one?" I asked.

"Yes, only one."

Woo-hoo! I thought. I'll glide through my senior year.

That didn't happen. Instead, I sputtered to the finish line.

English, as taught by Mr. Reynolds, was like constructing the United States Constitution. It was the most grueling writing experience that I have ever endured.

"Tracey," he said, as he handed me my redlined book report for the umpteenth time, "you can do better than this."

"But Mr. Reynolds," I argued. "I've worked half a semester on this."

"Consider yourself lucky then, Tracey," he replied. "You have half the semester remaining to correct it."

"But all of your red marks are confusing me," I told him. "I can't figure out how to change it so you will like it."

"Change it so *you* will like it, Tracey," he responded. "This is your work. You need to paint a picture of this book with your words. Proper sentence structure, spelling, and punctuation are essential, too. Imagine you are Mozart, Picasso, and Hemingway all wrapped into one. Keep at it, Tracey. You can do this."

Nathan O. Reynolds, a lifelong educator who took immense pride in the success of his students, set the bar high for everyone. He passed away peacefully at his home in Los Angeles on June 26, 2019.

If I could speak to him today, I would say, "Thank you, Mr. Reynolds. It has taken me forty-four years to finish that book report and I finally like it."

Rest in Peace.

Wondering

Writing 100 slice of life stories is no small feat. Unfortunately, one of them was rotten so I tossed it out. My green banana memoir has revealed snippets of my life that resonate with many of you. I'm flattered beyond words. Now I am contemplating whether this exercise should come to an end or not. My life, of course, will go on. My love of writing will not wane. But maybe this was just an experiment to justify sharing my stories with someone other than my husband. I am grappling with this as I type.

Every day a story presents itself whether we have the capacity to capture it with words or not. I pay close attention to what goes on every day. I listen to my inner voice and those of people around me. To be clued-in to the day's events is to be present, alive, connected. These are qualities I was born with.

I have always been an observer of my actions and words. As I write this short essay, I cannot say with certainty that I will post again each week as I have done thus far. If my outreach has been effective, then more of you will tune in to the extraordinary occurrences that spring forth every day and capture them in the best way you know how. That would be my greatest reward in having written 100 stories for you. Well, almost!

Thank you all for reading *I Don't Have Time for Green Bananas.*

ABOUT THE AUTHOR

Writer, poet, and humorist Tracey Fuller is the author of two published short stories about her mother-in-law, Barbara. Short Édition, a French publishing house selected Tracey as its first American writer to be featured in their Short Story Dispensers that are housed in public spaces throughout the world. She splits her time between Rancho Mirage and Carlsbad. Jim is always by her side.

Acknowledgements

I would like to thank my husband Jim for the love, patience and compassion he has shown throughout the writing process and express how valued I feel being his wife for over 38 years. What once was marvelous, still is.

Many thanks to my daughters and their husbands for being such good listeners while also offering moral and technical support whenever needed. A special shoutout to editor Julie Wenzlick for organizing these stories into a book that I am so proud to share with family and friends. Your efforts are much appreciated.

-Tracey Fuller

www.ingramcontent.com/pod-product-compliance
Lightning Source LLC
Chambersburg PA
CBHW042016090426
42811CB00015B/1660